Contemplation, Deliberation

B O B   C A R E Y

authorHOUSE

AuthorHouse™
1663 Liberty Drive
Bloomington, IN 47403
www.authorhouse.com
Phone: 833-262-8899

Published by AuthorHouse 12/01/2022

ISBN: 978-1-6655-7539-3 (sc)
ISBN: 978-1-6655-7547-8 (e)

Library of Congress Control Number: 2022920966

Print information available on the last page.

*Any people depicted in stock imagery provided
by Getty Images are models, and such images are
being used for illustrative purposes only.
Certain stock imagery © Getty Images.*

This book is printed on acid-free paper.

CONTENTS

PREFACE

When I feel my work on thinking what to write has ended, I see tomorrow and here I am challenging myself to have a discussion between the heart of mind and the mind of the heart. Somehow, like a sparrow inside me, reasoning and prayers find a home on these pages written with a calm hope to succeed. With a push and a tug from out of darkness and into light. If this isn't enough to know, I may debate in a spiritual side of me by knowing my heart knows me. As interwoven be the days and years in me, the vlave of trees in the meadows 6f thought about me, I shall maintain curiosity of where peacefulness runs her innermost flowers over the clouds of reality.

Let's keep in mind there is hope to know what is best to be. We are beside a mountain with a meadow within. Truly, about life signs point toward a beginning of knowing and hopefully not losing compassion in my feelings brought to words. Where my guidelines are senseful it is good to be thankful for living in this country I don't settle for one idea as me while I set my goals to have an inner belief upon God is shore of goodness. It is my prayer you find seriousness and awareness within the pages ahead.

When peace of mind is hard to find, may seem a relief needs a pathway to take to find someone special to give a caring smile. This is a blessing in need of a smile. To receive is to give back then love is recognized. We all need to hold onto our senses when sadness is near. My answer is to escape to poetry about life's pathway where coconuts are eaten, not for falling on the head. Let's let Jesus take us where goodness is a feeling to have. We all have to face any situation and pray where the vallies of the soul appear to the mountains all beheld as dear. The mind may have enough to deal with so realize a new prayer with the light within, the one of forgivnance. Pages like flowers come and go. When a butterfly opens a good feeling inside asking for nature to be inside I know mysteries can help feelings in finding one's self. We need be humbled in prayer. We can realize to be part of nature is to find hills inside and about, all for peaceful paths to be on. To dwell upon happiness is to be blessed by the ways of kindness while we need wisdom to settle for a clear mind and appreciate the love miracles hold.

People need pray as much as people need people. Let there be trust in an honest way to be. To be honorable in God's giving is to do one's best asking little yet growing in His love. Why God's nature to people is because we all prayer, forgivnance and to be part helping out someone when they are distressed. Don't feel lost for there is peace inside and a spirit to guide. When all seems hopeless, this happens, don't be lonely or upset, find someone you can believe in.

When we learn to look at a lot of gains we can find peace... the vision of living a life can be better. Don't get lost as in a depth of reasoning even I can find purpose even when my life I be does not make sense for now. Then all seems hopeless and wrinkles too I try not to be hopeless, keep a Bible nearby. Feelings so given; feelings so blessed, truth has got it life is still as the prayers we know in us. As life seems to find a faith in an inward glow of how to be the best hold onto yourself, find truths in happiness. Peaceful waves coming toward the shores of the soul looking for courage to begin each day by finding a love of a special moment beneath this spiritual skies of Jesus. When the eagle lands upon his nest, truly the nature of things is better. My trees of thought may sway in the breeze I find a logical pathway before I am underneath the moment of nature I didn't know. Did not know today yesterday. Could not know how to find my rest and how to believe and know lives are equal, life is fair. Fairness is a hope we all like to find, but life doesn't seem fair everyday. If you are fair with yourself, you just got to be fair with yourself. If you think life is too much to be, life, prayers are answered and one is to gather oneself and take on the path God wants you to find for there has to be logic in living when life begins to make sense.

To have a song in our hearts, a melody of grace, a more than just a feeling of love for God and blessings to be thankful to know. To what purpose God gives us is to find an expression so fitting and proper inner lights are presents enough for goodness to be firm in ways of asking for forgiveness, salvation and a hope for we all need love.

To have a love for people, a feeling of love for God finding a properness to grow each day in His love. We need to reach out to have a purpose as properness of good expression of self can be always aware, noticeable and feelings can be explainable. To listen to hear where one's thoughts are with a love for life in a respectful and a kindly endeavor life may be. Why poetically people look inward is where prayers are answered, peace is found. With an acceptance of self, we all try to be in a helping manner, careful, yes, yet always growing inside the heart.

To be firm in thanking blessings. Be kind, peaceful and let every moment be a love for life. Tears may fall, challenges may become upsetful, so keep hope to better life and in this manner, happiness may be around the bend. There may be many paths to follow, more ideas to see yet don't forget to be serious and concerned like Jesus must have seemed. This outlook, this belief in others may seem a pathway to always inside to become tolerant and kind. Problems will happen, so we should be brave, hold one's head high and be proud as answers are with goodness life can find for there are miracles that make things right. Give time for the soul to be just spirited enough to help sadness by looking for peace, not confusion.

Times will be less contemplated, less confused and we got to think how with God's love circumstances will improve. Let memories be of religious days where thoughts seem prayers in so many ways. And we all feel why's and because's make sense, lessons so sad and abrupt end up a pat on the back. Work days end.

When there is sadness there may be racing thoughts that disturb the heartbeat of all of what went wrong. When a person looks at the entire picture there may seem distress and this could lead to despair. When this does happen call on a friend to help, remember any situation of days past in a hope to explain where the real problem is and why turmoil set in place 1·rhere momentary grief need be gone and a mental band aid is all that is needed to be alright again. With a prayer, truth now sees a meadow of goodness where a band aid is the best that could be and all should be even enough to believe. As trying to explain a sorrow usually is difficult to be when a mental wound happens, in its place is a lot of rhymes of poetic understandance where all now seems that was sad is now understanding the entire picture. This sunset may even be a better person by explaining life is not always a bowl of cherries. This newly found envisionment finds peacefulness in prayer and encouragement to become understood and a better person in the ways of understanding oneself and awareness of how to be... people help people and become thankful when times are taught.

Nobody likes harsh lessons. To believe inside is to get up and learn life is gentle, so hope that when problems arise, be brave for some lessons may need that poetic band aid. I find there is logic to trying one's best. Tranquility is good to have.

As lost as a person can seem, I will be an effort to society to let these pages not only to be entertaining, but bring out distress and try to turn it into happiness. Where anxiety is a state of mind, let's all find logic to grow flowers on hilltops so as not to be hurt again. We all should be caring people. Let1 s give, even ourselves; a strong benefit of the doubt. If life has endless streams of the spirit, I like anything, remember to stay afloat. As at the end of problems is, could seem a little weariness. To know one's thoughtful mind is alright, mighty fine.

As a new morn approaches, the heart plays harps and the mind spends much time simply being thankful, yet learned that some actions are difficult full of errors all needed to be seen. A pathway to a purposeful life is to know it's alright to re son out a problem. There may be only a candle that flickers in the cold as we have to look for an answer and realize it's always been near. A candle's flame helps explain the singer's song.

To have an active mind full of kindness is best and talking matters helps get rid of regrets. To prevent great sadness, some people risk more than their sanity. Some circumstances are explainable, some are not. Still, come judgment day, everyone good is innocent of being upset if we are acceptable to see inner prayers answered. Let's think positive and trust our neighbor.

Learn to appreciate life, not to put all your time in being less than sober. Let's make our own pathway and have a mental roof to take it upon yourself to have time for thought. Don't feel sad at day's end. Try not to cry, have a blank face nor be fearsome of tomorrow. Let's let the pages of the heart, mind, spirit and soul look into life's spelling out of itself being ever so thankful to the Savior whom pulled me away from crutches. Prayers are better than not, more to be... prayers answer problems, prayers are free.

Patiently we need know ourselves, be of admiration for a friend, to gather symbols like sea shells in a jar where tears are not always sad. Like a songbird sings knowing more than inner happiness we need be best calm, of kindness and prayers. Try to expressions be poetic and little waves of thought knowing there is a way to be like words reaching out for the place. Of certain feelings, emotions and love for Jesus to help finding a home in the heart. We need to be known as part of a song is to gather love's innerness and reach for the stars.

People need never doubt themselves. When I fear for my sanity, I find my trustworthy pen and remove the problem. Regrets I can do without. Courage is a good trait to have if a situation can't be handled by niceties. Wherever our canoes paddle us, to have goodness in helping people eventually the picture does become, never completely often forgotten yet forgiven. The circles of one's personality lost, will return.

While an open heart seems to give way to an open mind, where we all need friends to gather parts of our soul and spirit is a good reason why we are put on Earth. Living in kindness is to find how great life can be. Let our struggles be our peace of mind. While fairness is not always a happy task; may be very rude, they should end up blessings in disguise. What makes trust and truth makes sense. All upsetting ways need have an end. Life is an open book. If someone turns an important page, this may find peace of mind upsetting and struggling to see exactly what can take from a normal state of mind. Those mind storms may seem years of sleepless nights. During daylight a rainbow will come, that of a new beginning. I put away sorrows with prayer that causes miracles. Let peace find a little more understandance each day, see the spirituality breath, gather wisdom and let's have high hopes be on solid ground. With prayers and peace of mind with endlessness of thoughtfulness inside, one's heart comes more content, sanity proves there are windy forests talking of thankyous the best they can. These lessons, like much in life, are difficult yet were more than escaping into naps.

Where I will be years from now I do not know. Perhaps inside a mental cave where poetic, symbolic waves bath my soul. Perhaps I will be sitting on a swing of kindness, a proper way to be. Enough memories have been in the lost and found, why books are read and want to make sense; let's not upset. Let's be of riddles and rhymes. We need find blessings in where doubts once were, in a big place, we need pray all the time. Let's believe in life and pray love comes.

I believe to think is to firstly listen to the poetic nature of the spiritual heart and soul. To be the best one can be, firstly contemplate what pathway you're on, deliberate upon all senses, realize a goal and pray to understand what changes in a predicament should or not become common place. Taking life seriously is the first step of a lifetime of belief in oneself. With ideas and ideals truths have no end. To pray for an answer of a problem may take days or years to be content with life. With morals unblemished, a new day will have designs always there yet not to known be until one thanks Jesus for blessings received. One is never lonely with Jesus remembered in one's very actions and deeds. As all divine truths lean on one another giving lessons. Good thoughts are everywhere if only we find time to pray. If I tumble, well feelings are included in an upset way we pray for a smile enough to return to that goodness that might of been. There are similarities noticeable between a cloud and a good book. Rain will end, so does a book. Let's all think over the nature of life, the nature of awareness.

I am a thought waiting to be, a question wanting an answer, a duty I am asked to have and a theory wanting to fly away to take a chance of explaining the wind. I am not important if I forget·\That is right or wrong. However if I forget a problem I might become sad until I take the minus and turn it into a plus. My plus is to be myself is to do my best.

INTRODUCTION

In the depth of wisdom, with all the glory life can bring, unto the worship of our living Lord and foreverness in our hearts and mind I have hope and prayers that lost thoughts and words will be found. While freedom beholds a lot, peace has slow seen feelings of truth and honor. This is found within the logic of belief in Jesus. Our grace of thoughtful thinking finds in the mist of Love for Jesus to maintain honor, trust and respect. Prayers for a better life for all takes patience. To do one's best is all anyone can do. There seems to be guidance in the mind. Feelings, emotions and even the learned guidance of one's heart all take their place when decisions are to be made.

Random thinking may not always be a final say or truth and one has to struggle to get by. He have to unconfuse oneself to find out there is righteousness inside and about in spirit and soul. Living in true stand peace of understanding and a good realization of the inner personality shows how poetic life can often be. This sling of contentment may be a smile not lost.

I am so fortunate to write. I explain my feelings and have purpose. I roam the meadows of thought and am thankful in many ways. Let's move away doubt learn to find love and be hospitable and free. Let Jesus be a place in our lives giving light and guidance while prayers are answered and contentment found. When forgivnance happens love is found. I untangle my past and watch confusion pass. When a secret place is found, I pray it appears worthwhile. Most thoughts are worthy of action. If one falls, gets up and see the tapestry we live for is a learning experience.

The traffic may confuse, leave one alone or lost for there must be an answer. To take one's heart seriously is when I see me open my heart as I try to find peace to give. To be of truth, to accept oneself leave contentment that is a smile of all is good. There comes meaning to life. I am constantly exploring my mind and where there is concern may be becoming a virtue of a beloved blessing. By trusting in Jesus we l earn to accept the duty life is.

As I describe a feeling of thought more than thought, I think about my actions and learn to believe in the paths I seek not to be emotional bumps yet some are. As sorrows some are unbearable, got those blessings of knowing a brother or a friend. As life is kind and good, we need be understood.

At times, life against the winds of thoughts and deeds can hurt. To exercise the mind and body in a positive way could let light enough within to walk away from stress and see a better path to take. Taking deep bountiful breaths should be finding prayers enough to smile problems away. To conquer emotional thinking leaves a clean thoughtfulness in a peace of one's very existance. Senseful thinking may not be fail proof. To let Jesus in one's heart is answer enough to problems. To have trust in a kindly manner is to encourage those spiritual skies of the heart and mind to give wisdom intertwined with peace to give a reassurance enough to be calm and tolerant weather rain or shine. My grammar may be lacking yet my heart is not.

To make sense is to live and accept Jesus and always keep respect to love and be loved in return. I have a peace in me that needs protect my love for God. I will never say good-bye to my religious beliefs making it easier to begin the morn with forgivnance and patience. To trust in Jesus is to find trust in oneself.

What is a mortal fabric if not made of threads? What is a song without a drummer? Do not we learn our poetic thinking by footsteps trying for meaning inside our beliefs? And what of truth? Does not being truthful for blessings and peaceful calm winds of the soul. The truth of thought may become a place inside as large thoughts might take a few years to be understood, satisfied with and keep going on. Little thoughts such as happiness may be so endless where moments give to a loved life. Do we imagine our dreams and all in the name of a real strong love of Jesus in us? Living may seem to reason, love of church, purpose and patience. To ignore these character traits is wondering how to be thankful for the presents life beholds. I try to keep happiness in my heart and know prayer helps.

I need always seem to find myself by writing descent paragraphs and having new objectives inside me. Rhyming thinking thoughts need not be confusing. I may often be. Living grows with love in an understanding way by tears and laughter, hopes and prayers. Let's say life comes from within. The courage, the determination and prayer have endless more attributes beginning with faith.

I hope not to change the true miracle life is, not to change the heart.

I respect all kinds of truths inside my life. Some truths need explaining. Most do help and stop heartache and do away with doubts. When mental clouds clear, feelings may take ever and begin a good life. To have good thoughts and being among friends gives peaceful memories. We all need learn different ways to be kind as prayer opens a window of not being lost. Let hope within grasp out for peace with Jesus and even learn to be thankful to living as we all learn to believe in reality.

Let there be light in a mental forest making a path to salvation. While darkness may be confusion; let the spirit take over in prayer and, every day find peaceful ways to see oneself. It is how we grow in respect to one another to appreciate and prayerful for blessings and learn from mistakes, living all makes sense. The proper way to be is where teachings of life bring friendship with Jesus.

It is upmost important to be oneself. Most people look for solitude. So, in our comings and goings let's not be foolish. Where proper explanations may seem many tomorrows away, with love in your heart most depressions leave and here comes a senseful disposition. Explaining oneself takes time. So we laugh and cry.

Every day of my life I am not a success. I expect failure I pray the days be happier than loneliness is. Even in the darkest of nights, when our hearts have trouble finding light, we need heal our hearts by just chasing away sadness. Light, even a little candle in the heart helps the spirit to be free. I tend to hold to this for understandance is a good step to solve a dilemma. As fish may feed people, I feel small to all the enlightment abound as I struggle to be someone. We all need be more inside our hearts and minds to be.

I am concerned of where my heart takes me. What do I do when the sound of wind and rain do not appreciate or want any part of? Should I escape the winds of torment or accept a challenge to change whom I am? I know life often seems not fair. All I know to do is light a candle, pray and hope innocence does pull through the darker times. Let's believe in a strong spiritual life for all the good people to take command and serve what they believe in. There is not a song I cannot hear, a vison of hope I can find, a prayer I can take seriously as I think it is an endless task to believe in oneself. If confused, read on and simply seek courage to turn pages and fall not where I have fallen. While some truths might find corners to hide in, do sweep mental rooms for they need periodical sweeping too.

I am alone. The weight of my living heart knows I need prayer. I pray tomorrow my faith will be good enough, not shaken, with a clear mind watching my thoughts and always knowing to trust Jesus. As other doubts of life seem on their way we need prayer for logical paths to be. Unto all my life in the past, I look for cobwebs hiding. It seems a mystery, mostly even unseen, yet to take a positive outlook is the only way to truly think about life. I don't mind being hugged, I hope they are many and not too harsh. I have feelings found in the wayward winds of prayers. Now I feel I find in me a wizard of endless explanation and a daylight of trusting my mind not to race around yet is manner of hope. No one is more than a dawn of why peace knows and seems finding oneself and a few thoughts of love and an unconfused, sober light in everyday so blessed on Earth.

We are to find the joy in living, to be a circle of inspiration unto one's entire self, to recognize sadness as having some tears and prayers. For people in need is to realize they need better sense of their lives. Life needs to know what should become of oneself. Patience never is to get upset. There are a lot of paths, one may find if one thinks of how to be. What is poetry?

To everyone, to teach one is to let matters of past be better off today. Truths foreseen, logic not forgotten and Jesus pointing toward salvation can see a winded mind turning to be calm. With a trust in oneself is a newly found way to be, with a love for Jesus, poetically found within. We all need one another if only to gather up moments for prayer. Love inside oneself conquers all. So much is in the meadows of the soul that sometimes I feel thoughtfulness as peaceful for all. Let's all be careful not to forget the miracles life is and run for to be a person of faith, love and tranquility.

Some lessons are as simple as eating pie while others may seem to leave me in the middle of a desert and not knowing why or how. My entire being seems is a struggle to know, to understand life. One's perception may seem to be a moment hinting of tomorrow today in a simple way. In the midst of our being is a flute, a song of the babbling so realized that our personal prayers are finding answers. There and a lot of places are peaceful days and the inward self finds Jesus a reality, not a dream.

Personally speaking, I am happiest when I dwell upon empty pages and realizations come out helping thoughts be. A sunset, a sunrise or a rest in the meadows at day's end. The goodness of expression should not end. I may falter, even slip. Only praying may find tomorrow when I feel sad or somewhere lost. I look for truths to me. I hope my thoughts are waterproof; some ideas may be a mirage. I look for a great day when there are ideas that find me at peace and all feelings are meant to be. Explaining the spiritual soul helps me find Jesus behind kindness making helping what is best to be. And so what is best seen takes my heart and mind to understand realities. Life may seem unfair and upsetting. The best logical thinkers may fall sometimes. To regroup and find there is light enough to think things over is to set sail in a calming, spiritual and meaningful recognition of how to become more than what hurt, to receive the gift of understanding not all for awareness wins most disputes.

If I am going to do my best, I have to basically try to be myself always beginning to go where I want to struggling a little and praying a lot. We are all in this boat called life, full of any trust we hold dear, left in peace with God where mental storms are outlawed. I hope not to lose my place nor forget that I'm doing. I am on a kind chair with all freedom of expression of contemplating my thoughts and deliberating what be the best words to explain unto sturdy shores of existence. With courage in my heart and soul, I try to understand what is religiously waiting to take place. Prayer, love and kindness and hopefulness are the symbolic keys the mind to lead the way to freedom. There are alot of tomorrows waiting to be an explanation of my why's about thinking and wherefores of logic within just waiting to grow poetic flowers of a sincere love and kindness always. We all need carefully be aware of how we are thankful for the affection life brings. Often enough to listen to one's heart is the best to collect goodness as to be serious to others and to oneself. By emotional peace, fewer stumbling blocks are found. Those that are seen as on a pathway need be made the best way to deal with.

The sight of the soul that explains blocks may take only a request to smile in a prayer to know there is help.

To better oneself is not just for oneself. When life seems not happy or sad, we must find a balance to see recognizable theories that are helpful and generous not only to oneself.

There are many tomorrows that daylight everywhere will bring peace within; it is good to think good ideas and thoughts if only to protect your feelings. A matter for or of the mind is where to answers, solve dilemmas by knowing the causes and effects to life may take a lot of love and good books to inside be strong and see one can be assured in one's comings and goings.

On a march through the forests of regrets I wait ever-so patiently taking care to be, do and think what is right and hope for a sigh of relief. Now I feel my heartbeat one at a time, one to the next. Sadness does happen. In these paragraphs, I have a secure feeling as inner trust may sometimes take time as often it is to live up to other's opinion of what should and not be. As the spirit calms, a new found strength of character no longer dwells in a sad way.

Please don't find me a little saddened as unto Jesus Christ, just be yourself. As tedious as thought can get, as a fracture does heal. Having purpose is found in many directions even when down a passage that; for a moment does not make sense. Take time, look about and around and all is done; better because you and I care too much. One's total environment may seem or be nice. Let's make the best of what we got. For now, I suppose I learn from my past with peace and patience abound.

Asking to become a clown but remembering to be a content person with a smile. This has a lot of truth to know of oneself, a lot of tears never there for all the clowns one knows will never really take off their make-up. There is more effort than before when life was an emotional struggle and between the waves within where seas small seem large and not only one's heart yet what is in one's mind and soul. This guides one's innermost spirit to find out where there are happier days in the manner of trusting oneself, knowing courage is in there where clowns throw paper water. We all have only our hearts to become our guide. I believe in more than what I write, read or say. Always in the often-felt presence of lovely roses, the gardens of thought are where our imagination helps find them. I will stumble on the pathway of soul and spirit trying to bring rest to a sometime-troubled mind. I seek patience as not to fall yet accept the fact I am not alone, not on an island. I need an occasional coconut to fall on me and seek out wisdom's tree to find hope the desert when mentally parched and just know that a lonely rose is better than no rose at all. There's awareness in God, within our being where trusted truths of a love for life.

Where a rose is where depression is not. Where prayers need be answered soon and all hope is more than a day is as years fall into a meaningful rendition of loving Jesus. Jesus, a name worthy of bringing daylight within. Let there be prayers in our dreams for all fellow man. Why the days are in a manner of trust is why the friendly ways of trusting oneself may see there is a lot of peaceful acknowledgement of knowing oneself. There are no ends to the is part of the divine triumphant love of God is where all hope to be. Our hearts and minds work to seek courage to become helpful for a home. I realize in my heart there is a home. I realize in my heart there is a home bringing peace and serenity as prayers of the entire self will be answered. Years then fall into meaning of a love for Jesus.

While I am not a milky way for and of light. I know there is a peace for all in society. The circles of thought have no real end. Let's be a prayerful, sober and loving way as to look about and have our own nature. Let's dust away those cobwebs out of the window calls an awareness of hearing and bringing about any inner secrets I am finding to be proud or not for time catches the quickest runners. There may be a poetic bulldozer to dig out the soul, but I will.

BEGINNING THOUGHTS

Glory of life holds only one heart, the heart of the mind. Let's look for a better way to be from inward seas of touching ways to gathering acorns for Winter's cold. When we turn our attention to the actual resting place we are given, that this be reasonable is a gift not to be taken easily. When there is a peaceful sigh as years go by, while life revolves around the sun of inner vision... we all should take a moment of reflection and find there is a way to be thankful for our blessings and grow into love of God. I, about me, I am not what I see in a mirror yet how I present myself to my friends. My heart and mind may become more respectful to my belief in spirituality.

Within the realms of sanity, about the spiritual sky are angels of thought waiting to describe how to land those poetic ideas so they may be discussed. To struggles be life. Life, the lessons of learning whom one is and how he wants to be, here is a vision wanting to be know, even in the soul. I don't always make perfect sense of whom I am. The pathways of life may leave me lost. Even these pages may seem to me sand castles washed away by the waves of time, yet not supposed to be lost.

I keep my feelings from being lost at sea. If I have a chance to be a caring person, I will do such. People do need people, no doubt about that. Be sure of yourself. Let there be peace. Let there be prayers.

As we all l earn from one another we need accept what is proper as a thought or idea from someone is part of the joy of nature. Why does this become muchly not forgotten is here is a certainty in oneself to keep an open mind and heart, to find there is peace in prayer and life becomes a joy to know. Silently goes the rivers of the heart giving vessels of a warm feeling in the name of Jesus and all His love. Sometimes life can seem despair. If Jesus cares for me, I become thankful and thoughtful. Problems are not left in shadows yet brought to find no more a problem. Then people become safe within, can see through the rain and harvest good will and there is light inside the heart. Feelings for others are blessings not lost and known by Jesus as kindness. To find thoughtfulness is everywhere one may scratch a little of one's heart and know all the things possible. Then one's health becomes one with heart and mind and getting in a good emotional state for living needs an understanding of Jesus. Giving kindness in prayer is one-step for acceptance of self. It may take time to find oneself the way you'd like to be and problems may arrive. Doing one's best is always fine. Then look for peace of mind. To forget that Jesus does work in our lives is to be a little lost. To be looking for blessings is to find there are mental vallies of peace is to get up and see we all need faith in God -for tears dry and thankful for whom one becomes is to keep the mind thinking and open to see everything was alright in the first place.

It is normal to have ideas yet don't forget to take time to be thankful for love that never leaves our hearts. Feelings can become upset yet when they do take time to realize not all is as bad off as it seems so we apologies.

Let's be thankful to the children that put a smile on our faces, bring forth a certainty of self and stuff our hearts with a thoughtfulness not forgotten. No words are good enough to discuss life.

We know for we think. We really need believe in Jesus more than whom we are. By kindness, most all trusted truths are found. It may take a long time before an upset day explains what is going on, why a mental roof leaks and the spiritual sky smiles at one's heart and most all seems explainable. There is soon a goodness nobody can take away. When nowhere is where one is left, seek a Bible, soon all is fine.

Without any remorse, another day begins. We need learn not to f all again, not to place yourself away from society. I challenge words when it comes to thinking of how to make sense of myself. Thoughts can change like the weather so I kick the bucket of sadness away and work for a better day. Most people have sadness in life when all seems upset. Let us not sit idly by and seem to fall apart. We have to remember whom we are to know what pathway we take and not jump to conclusions. What is thought may or not be true. We all hope we have friends of kind ways. Friends that hold hands in mental calm is really something to see. It all is like finding prayer in a storm, peace in a prayer.

With an idea or something to go by, I feel I can go forth into the parts of my life and see what a tear of happiness is. Give as music in words and feelings all dance in love of being part of a larger picture. A picture where the heart in my chest skips a beat.

Putting hopes onto faith is to thank little blessings no matter how small. Having faith is praying and even trusting yourself. We all should battle sadness by blessings of goodness and thanking clarity of one's soul. Think upon all aspects of decisions that may guide. Let kindness received from living kept and even helping someone. Songs are in me, a part of my life not to leave yet a blessing unto feelings becoming explained.

It is often good to let Jesus help us find our way. The Messiah helps thought to be; a mind to encompass what was not and points loneliness to be a prayer. It may be difficult to find what has not found light. We learn to respect being acceptable to oneself accepting and giving smiling in a kind way. As days will be, and be they may, my mind discuses with my heart what to be and when.

Timeless energy inside the heart, winds whistle unto the meadows without a tear, settlements grow without fear... butterflies run in flight like love's song remain untouched. The entire self feels alright asking for acceptance of the stars often seen to be where a stream jumps about under God's sun. With kindness and adoration life can be, realities' realizations have no begin or end. We are like thoughtfulness believed highly in. To think unto oneself and how life could be find what is lost past is to find realizations acceptable.

We listen and learn of God's lesson to love yet never completely grasp all that is meant to be seen, accepted and become more faithful unto God's love and part of eternity.

Prayers, praised as a peace unto the vallies of the mind, we can find, keep a simple memory in our thoughts, realize there is light in the mind, seek courage to remind our peaceful ways of why we all appreciate there are hopes in a sense of feelings where once were doubts. Doubts of what seems sad may or may not find much to be concerned with, only a prayer to seek courage in a smile where life is always worthwhile. Trust begins in a daylight of love, a proper way to do things the way they, knowing oneself; believing in oneself and letting love show itself in the comings and goings with Jesus inside one's heart. There is more of a chance to believe in oneself, where courage need be acceptable to religious beliefs.

Loveliness is a matter for or of the mind to find and recognize a place past materialism entering the spirit of giving as nature looks on.

To find a smile is to give a crust of bread to a friend. This is not only helpful yet fulfilling to body and mind. No matter where you stand, giving helps one to accept oneself. I think on all sides of life from spiritual sides to the material sides. I climb an imagined hill until it is real. By effort in oneself, there finds faith.

With respect to good people around me, in a parade of thoughts are words from inside, I respond to logical moments, find truth in communication with my soul.

By the truths of our past, our beliefs and our duties one needs a certainty of self. Brave be the heart, the sky of the mind to gather oneself unto endless years is to know where to think how to be. The past becomes the best of the present, the shadows loose to light and a grace of self-expression is found. There becomes a certain responsibility while knowing friends. One should know how to morally stand, how to seek a certainty in what is said. With peace, an understanding path could become clear.

As age is found, understanding oneself brings a way to grasp onto the soul. Being thankful, we all need learn to accept the love of Jesus. Let truth and love find a peacefulness like meadows with lakes where swans show love is a freedom in the heart and soul. Holding onto one's belief in goodness there.is respect for God.

Lost as thought can become, I place my canoe of happiness unto my prayers hoping to find logic in myself. No sinking canoes in my heart. Only drums nearer than before. As I jump hurdles of often learning where to be, there I find a ladder to understand how to open up and know there is Jesus will point the way as not to be lost.

Memories are funny things... they may awaken one in a sleep. Problems may seem to be like verifying this or that or searching for what can be a gain or not or end up knowing how to figure that memory out. When sad emotions find their place to realize one, this may hurt, be a disgrace so running inside a corner happens. The corner may be a friend. The object lesson is to look, find and be part of the goodness of life. If it is, one thing after another and tears to a friend's concern may be nicer to be.

To get help is no disgrace. To look to find oneself is to seek happiness along with reality. With as much as a prayer can be, it is best to be thankful as friends known as a gift from the love of Jesus. Simple be the heart Jesus sees and gives a patient love in an understanding there is freedom to become answers for what is best. The solution of circumstances that don't work out may seem sad. Be this a tear, a loss let the spirit guide accepting the end of a problem.

Whisper do the four winds of thought to place in the forgotten way and find goodness to be where the poets express a new day, and be thankful to move a doubt to be no more. It is true we all learn from life and unfortunately, problems happen.

With the art of writing, I say my conscious mind is open to see so people don't get lost in bad poetry. We all need l earn how to pray and by doing so, tomorrows will be greeted by the best we can be.

Have the daylight be as kind as the kindness in you. While keeping together, heart and soul, a song in your heart for unto Jesus and God words are thoughtful paths to see what was sad may be a little hurt, for prayers stop sadness and hopefully love fills the empty space. While peace of mind is hard to know, a relief of sadness is remembering Jesus cares. He cares for the lonely giving relief by blessing life is.

Life, how does one take the sadness it can be? Where is an answer for true peace of mind? Sadness, not being nonsense, needs be gone for soon is sense;'soon is love, peace and all that be kind. With every instinct of life explored, there is God to listen to any situation that presents itself. There are valleys and mountains all about they are dear, for here is refuge from the living ways that can take their toll with a new prayer for the love of forgivnance. As goodness is like leafs on trees, I pray my alertness helps my poetic butterfly to unfold nature and let innocence become prayer.

Because years await in a mystery, no reason why people can't plan ahead to remain sane even when undone by a storm.

What happens to oneself is most the time what one decides. It is a little sad when life is not fair or right. We can realize to make life better is all anyone can do. It may take more than what seems, more than one poetic ocean to find peace of mind. To make the sense of a situation is often not to get involved with what is not your business.

To dwell upon happiness is to be blessed by the ways of kindness one finds, sees inside oneself, l earns to gather wisdom to have a clear mind, sadness leaves when on a safe pathway. It is best to always have hope. Let the daylight reach out to one's spirit and soul for prayers are answered everyday. People need prayer as much as people need people.

Let's not let thinking ramble away. First, find a friend in Jesus, for He finds nobleness within the good of living. Belief in Him has no end. Let God's nature be held as dear. Brighten someone's day and your's will find peace.

Why the goodness of life is why books are written why people have an openness within, why love has honesty and there is a seriousness and a smile as we help and are helped. Where there is darkness, Jesus lights a candle of faith giving a new found belief in oneself. Why prayers are important is a place the child I was still is.

Living on an island is liie age and wisdom is. Al so to know a knowledge that there is a spiritual sky not so far away. Unto what is or may not become acceptable for unto my soul is thought I know is as me. No one can take away my freedom of a love for my personal beliefs. The heart I have is a love for not to being hidden. We may resume a lot of prayer, a basket full of love, a light from our personalities unto what is best is done. Do I more unto the light of believing in myself or hide under covers to the fear of tomorrow waiting to interrupt my train of thought? It is by my controversial me to me that I debate with my knowing ability and feelings. The respect I give to the vision I have of me is like a sparrow in a nest, then a builder of belief in the little way my mind knows to give.

CHAPTER ONE

A Stuffed Clown

Truth, both easy and difficult. What does it take to go where all is truth? What should be is never completely true f or tomorrow may open a curtain of new ideas worthy of exploring. No matter how much a person does, there are more paths to follow, more ways to be like flowers, some accepting now as truth, others are seeds waiting for their time to be.

As Stuffed Clown travels to many circuses giving smiles, laughter and being special with make-up. I am like a clown, full of thoughts waiting to smile unto the pages of life both spoken and written. A Stuffed Clown, he talks with make-up that expresses his love with smiles or frowns giving a lot at the circus, I imagine it's difficult to take off his face and often difficult to rest.

Without much, a clown has only make-up away from under the tent. Send a few roses to a clown, they can find a pathway in their hearts, a path that lets and helps the purpose, meaning and admiration of life be a smile. Clowns help civilization be good and worthwhile. I have learned to remember special times in my life. Some are serious, some I seem to laugh and learn from but I never forget how a clown takes away tension and leave me calm. When the circus is over, poets will, singers shall sing and we all seem to be happier about life. I can't thank a clown enough for the love a clown gives. God bless him.

Perhaps the are other pathways to take, dream about or make real if possible. Crossing a bridge may often be found as a way of kindness. I love my life, yet if I know there are often sad bumps in the road. If I can explain sadness, perhaps it is easier to take.

To give back blessings received may take awhile, however, it is best. We all need to make sense of ourselves. It is only by doing one's best in necessary ways first is how not to put yourself above others. Life may be very difficult to understand so we all need be considerate of our fellow man, thankful to extend a helping hand and keep thoughts of Jesus close. To believe inside oneself is to take care being sufficiently kind.

We may walk around in circles to learn more about our lives. By and by, what is a mystery hiding in one's mind is where wonderment gives way taking a prayer to search for kindness no more. When make-up comes off, a clown becomes a person too as we all need learn from each other. A clown really never says good-bye for those memories don't leave and our frowns will leave as a peaceful light is seen within the galaxies of the soul.

The spirit of life is endless as we all should find peace in the vallies of the soul waiting for love to guide our hearts. Let moments of decisions of where to go be noble, peaceful and part of society's manner of being friends with a clown, Jesus, God and family. To learn to trust oneself comes before believing in oneself. To see the way one's life is or becoming is like seeing a star glistening in the sky. To share a star with a friend may give different viewpoints of how to be, for good friends are hard to come by. We walk to run, run to rest and look for love though stars are nice. Everyone thinks different, most the time. As a child, we need see eye to eye.

To learn to trust yourself, firstly one needs to feel for others. This is a good inner light to have. Nobility is noticing the way one's life is becoming not forgetting forgivnance is a good blessing to know. Forgivnance for caring too much is a quest not to be over completely forgotten. We crawl to walk, walk to run, run to rest and look for love for love is best. The notions of thought may run amuck. When this occurs, have a good failsafe. Call it love. We all need to give our endless seas of love. This brings us closer in our private lives with Jesus. I try not to give too much love, love needs dimension, direction and good thoughtful, timeless meaning affecting oneself. Making a sanctuary and see we should not neglect, our hearts need mental guidance.

Smiles do have peace of mind. The kindness of one's heartbeat may become acceptance of oneself. Let's hope we all find our way in a boat of life asking for safety and not having a loose rudder nor rushing, being careful.

Senses of survival may need imagination when reality needs help. It all may seem a search from mental rooms of love, a passion to know a mention of thoughtfulness like a child's smile. With only one's heart, to bend a knee and pray for no wrong is to have peace in the vallies on one's soul. And so a stuffed clown shall be handshakes and hugs from love's shore bounded with the soul. For as difficult as life can be, we do not need to regret our way yet to be calm and find love is, always will be in childhood memories. To simply be oneself and with hope and dreams where liberty and honor find goodness contentment is seen. Just by being oneself, through good time and sad, peace comes.

When despair needs a dose of forgivnance, when one needs find a glimmer of hope… prayers may be a real good answer as we all try to run that last mile. Perhaps a new pathway needs to be explored for a change of attitude knows itself as necessary. Look for a near outlook. People need in their hearts and feelings to reach out and care for one that cries inside. Let's open eyes, look at the good, not sad anymore. With purpose to living is found and a grasp on oneself is an answered prayer. Because some people may be proud of the wav you lead your life, I have a feeling there are better reasons to improve, always.

And so, a stuffed clown smiles even the make-up is washed off and what is found, left to find is how to help others as you are helped. While an openness of self may at times get a little weary of past frowns, the levels of love given and somedays returned seem to need a certainty of belief of why one really is. While a peaceful rest may seem far, far away, rest may be a dream not seemed to be for the immediate tomorrow may become another frown. Why we go through a darkness is how we know people will be able to make candles and light a heart full of understandance. By this love, it is much easier to be among people.

While we open, see and try to understand life's'pages, why we learn and gain wisdom of how to see through a reflected self is where our stuffed clown sees his heart and soul lite rally becoming one. I feel if someone hurts me or is upsetting, I think of myself. Why daylight seeps through a window, why love runs to find trust, even when one falls again and again is where and why this poet has a pen. Whatever and why this poet has a pen. Whatever fits in those lines on faces and pages is when a song doesn't mind giving way to another and always one more. What is hope is a lot like a clown becoming a humbled person. That has been given, as a gift so much so, is when tears soon become a smile, both worthwhile. Remove a doubt, maybe a frown and find a joy in remembering when you're with someone you care for. When one is near someone loved, a lot is keeping circus memories nearby.

Remove a doubt, maybe a frown; see a joyful memory where feelings come to think of happiness. Now, then being a land of memories where inner thinking says love is why we are. Be people the ocean's tide of winded ways, like a sparrow in the hands of God not all too poetic for the winds of thought brush out the cobwebs of these souls and leave us friends with even ourselves.

A clown contemplates where to be whild deliberating what to do, how to be. To find a child with a frown, where saddened to tears, a clown may have not much time to help. Truly, a circus gives a loving light where there is sadness. Let's all find a sharing of blessings, pass our light to help someone by reaching out the best we know to. Reasoning has it to become of a certainty of happiness is to take life seriously. This helps problems not to be great. A good and decent feeling protects happiness and what is a trust may be years to earn if you are earned by effort and patiently be calm and peaceful. Let your spirit go on through the years. To share blessings is another smile of helping reaching and touching the best way toward understand and happiness. This should be taken as seriously as life itself. These feelings learn how to earn trust. Be calm. Find there are smiles we have and need as a certainty so strong passing all sad feelings is leading to prayer. With prayers, sincerity is best to be.

When there is prayer, let it be faithfully. Jesus takes life seriously, so we would do the same. The poetic mountains of thinking may seem never ending. While on the pathway of life, we all search for a purpose for our existence. As time passes so may our opinions go off in different directions. With the time spent well, it is easier to smile.

With a romantic flair, life goes on. Many good beliefs tag along. Let's be the health of reason with the ability to know wisdom as the light of God in us to see a fairness in spirit mind and always thinking what is best to do. Such becomes the smile of a clown as he hopes to give back the stuffing to find a newly found day of innocence and hope.

Us poor clowns go on, better for being in a circus tent, better for the smiles of loving ways, the recognition of the paper water, really was laughter. No one feels less a person when friends help an upset friend. This is good, this is best. To stop depression has a place as important. There are many ways to hold hands, to grasp the certainties of love and help them become realities of fairness of one's life.

If people care more for people, most problems leave. It is not a perfect World. A child growing up looks at the good in his life. When he sees not all is great, depression maybe a problem that lingers about. I prefer when mental blocks are moved to the side, find good feelings come to life inside an emotion of wordly ideas and thoughts. This real of strength may still need any madness explained, at least try to.

The question is what will be tomorrow? Let good and kind and descent people hold hands and work for a better day. We all want a problem free society. Until then, poets shall ponder their spirits and soul dreaming of how life could be free from grief and turmoil. We all should learn kindness and being gentle. Still some bruises take decades to heal. The alphabet I use has no surprises, but life does. As days, turn into years we may look a bout and only see sadness.

Most people have hidden turmoil inside. We know opinions, no matter how much based on fact, usually become lost in a desert storm knowing no other grace than fear. Fearing and knowing is one thing. Fear not thought about yet inside is totally another. That other could lead to chances away from normality. Could we ever find out more than we are politely taught? The sorrows of fears unseen yet present may become more tormented bringing doubts to society. There are people disregarding logic and treating some awful throwing away any feelings due to some kind of trash mentality and twisted logic. This is more than sad. It grieves us all whom believe in God when some life's happiness is too hurt to be. Let the gentle be strong.

To cleanse, sanctify and be childlike in a firm way is, of course, to believe inside oneself. There, in one's mind should be a calming, peaceful and thinking to become of saneness full of joyousness. Bringing the spirit to be to be triumphant, if not in one's room, inside the inner soul full of firmness and strength realized by circumstances hopefully good and kind.

It isn't sad to me to write. It was freedom and love that guided my heart. I hope life is a fight in such a way down the path of righteousness. Don't be forlorned or let years go by wasted. Some people pull rabbits out of hats. Yet, what can we do? Let's be aware of what can hurt. Let my mistakes be little, let my heart pure, let my soul be fair and let my spirit be free. As there is this within, let feelings be kind and all about. We all know when something is wrong. When one can't put words with a problem, maybe prayers can help. In fact, let's all try to help our fellowmen.

When I get nervous, I think of something to do. Just remove the soul from problems. This can bring out calmness, hope to be no problem to other and believe how indescribable life be. Let clowns in us still smile explaining what does and doesn't make sense until the spirit brings peace of mind. With the inner personalities we give, finding a friend and know to share, learn and find new viewpoints. It is quite important to get some involvement by accepting a friend as responsibility. While being of this goodness, a new love is found like a sunset waiting to be, all seems better than before.

When the sun sets, let it be on dreams that have started to become real with each passing day, to be a place of ones' hopes as to see a memory of clowns' teachings to smile as to be thankful for the stuffings of feelings waiting for realities. We need to look to set our mental and courageous sails to a place where there are good thoughts. Some thinking may become a poetic pottery, waiting to be put to poetic fires.

What becomes of a person where lonely be his deck of cards? Why should not one work to become more with himself. Are we forgiven for our unanswered prayers so other may hold onto their ways of desires in prayers? Let us all do better everyday in everyway. Even when one is heartbroken, even when there is sadness, hold your head up and hope that prayers are best to be, leave no one upset, find there is peace. Don't be embarrassed to ask for help if problems get too much to handle. Keeping firm with oneself is how to light wordful candles and pray for peace and hope within.

It is important to keep faith near. God often works miracles, miracles make sense. Never give up hope. We all have it in us to be thankful for blessings.

You've heard about having a warm heart. How about a mind warm with kindness? Decisions may be many, hopes may seem also. There may seem too many paths to take so let's be sincere in what we do. In a very giving way, understanding what is right or wrong is always best. When a white dove flies free, when a songbird sings, when the heart of my chest beats out of love, I know I am found to realize all is well if only in a dream of tomorrow. Lonely be man without God. Find a marble in your soul, let's see if the spirit will let it roll. Kindness be all anyone needs. Let's not fall down crying on the blocks of my mentality of my entire self. The skies one one's mind may have gray clouds when problems seem many, answers few. I love to expose profound feelings, put them into what is wordly, bring them out into the open, both good and sad thoughts. Noticing what could be sad before it is leaves problems easier to know, think about and life is easier.

It may take someone to come into your life. Choose someone kind and concerned. To be of a calm manner, to be healthy in body and mind is to have a good day where there is love to do better, in a love for Jesus. With love, struggling to be the best one can be and new kind of mental tictocs are found in one's heart. Heart thoughts may not always seem fair. Some may not seem fair. Thoughts may even fall into a realm of fear and this is in need of control. Sometimes in our lives we hold sadness in. Secrets may or not be best.

My stuffings are from my feelings. Some are of joy, some are sad. What makes life all worthwhile is a tree of faith more real with age. How a tree of faith comes to be is firstly with a simple thought. This thinking may be so beautiful, I want to write it out. The idea I may forget but I know the feeling is now. I see a kind of fertile where the thought may be as my pen stumbles across a seed. The seed grows as paragraph flows about the way of wisdom. Chapters put down a leaf at a time on faiths' branches. And the roots hold onto the soil of faith. Years become a pathway where nearby trees shade the soul in a respect to a love of God. To realize a thought as soil and seed is to gather oneself for a new day. As children, we glide our wooden planes. As adults, we can see them land. There are many struggles there be to find a perfect life. Yet struggles bring us blessings.

There are presents inside we receive, the one that rhyme yet need not for unto a whistling wind are prayers answered, peace found and we find there is love to gather, thought and look, there is a garden of trees. We all must have angels in our hearts that guide our paths and leave any questions answered and decisions can wait to be until done unto a debate and theories turn fact. Knowing ideas can become knowledgeable. Just like our poetic stuffed clown, wisdom may seem an endless river gong on forever and ever. When there is a tear in someone, there are prayers Jesus may answer, a poetic band aid is an answer.

Good band aids are church, the Bible, perhaps a movie. To meditate puts one in a gracefully gentle pathway and life gets easier to be and become. While times may be changing, how one is influenced, put forth demands of courage and rightful of beliefs felt certain about. If all there is are dreams, make a new pathway but most of all, don't get lost. While an openness can be a song in a dream, let's not forget the shores of reality.

I can't know what might linger in me like icicles on a roof, or days best dismissed and unattended ideas need proper thought. With the ending of a day, I do like to have proper thoughts. A stuffed clown wants goodness in all of us, realizations happy, tears to dry carefully. A good person knows how to be handling most situations and like a clown, trying always to keep a smile. We all have to realize it is our lives we must live. Keep the campfire of the soul alive; too many tears try not to find. Often prayers reach out. Let's not let prayers be just for oneself. Reach out. There are many ways to hug someone. Make friends in a way of peacefulness. There is love to living. Instead of getting upset, be considerate of others fiving a space to think things over. Over, like meadows of lifes' memories. Have understandance of others finding patience because not every single day is sunshine. Sometimes it rains. Don't be confusing to anybody, even yourself. Where there is a spank of nature, the water of the pond gives up the old catfish and the winds come again and ripples are felt in the heart and mind. Let's debate which way to turn, consult with the soul and be careful when you hear your heart. Let love be solid. I couldn't go to a clown asking for a big smile until for there is a need to present one well.

We all are clowns, or should be, in the way we would, so to speak, stand on our heads so someone dear won't fall down and get hurt. Choose the circles of spiritual side of mental health and the sun will set in a smile so near, so feelings become aware and rest for a new days is good, thoughts are better. Goodness and peace on the heart beating in an existence of importance is to be very careful on a certainty of whom one believes confusion no more. Realizations need be explored as reality holds hands with dreams. If we untangle the day as being differently well for night, all life's puzzles of thought become organized, some problems are easier to understand until tomorrow has an explaining manner.

Consciousness of thoughts, reality and prayer may guide the spirit so greatly, a soulful way to smile. With everyday that passes be there a lesson to find, there is a God that knows how to save lessons of how to know peace of mind, waiting for love of a mental window to see the subconscious guiding goodness of thought. I pray not to be nervous yet accept. Let the clown be a place to be within the thoughts of prayers and becoming thoughtful to others and oneself is to be descent and kind. Be acceptable and love life. Let the clowns bring beauty and effort to accept and let the heart guide, finding a smile like ripples in the soul for there is peace.

Make a castle of sand asking your hands to find a spiritual gathering that lasts in memory of past now in dreams. Perhaps only a clown can understand those questions where stuffings wait to be part of people's realities. There are many doors people do open, showing love and kindness with more tomorrows of thank you's what seem windy days where logic to know how to become prayerful works for a calmer mind. To be more meaningful is to have a logical heart of much kindness. I hope my life is filling time with a meaning acknowledgement seeking our courage to have a life of prayer.

Don't let a songbird stop singing even when living has a significant, kindly silence waiting for the next chapter of life to be reality. I have heard a canary sing and that is real beautiful. With a yearning to find a request for more castles by the seas of the soul, here comes the prayers of saints for Jesus to remind, to teach where the heart finds there is daylight within one's life and being. This is to seek poetry about life; nature beholds a lot more that than the mind can imagine. We whom have courage enough to find that the principle goal of life is to complete a day to be inspiration of care for others, to find years to brush out tangled sadness and be a man or prayer for life.

All the openness of the heart may be with a dawn if the realization we find of a duty to prayer is enough to be inside of every word of life's poetry. With all of nature talking loud, there are often patches made of love are needed to remind one of the goals we set may include a chance, life may be too much and one falls down by the wayside of thought itself. Where all of what can be is, no matter how one sees or what one feels, is a guidance factor for smiles may or may not come. So, after all, how can a clown make a smile until it is certain of kindness within. Let many poets build a strong heartful of love endearing. As a jellyfish has no scientific proof of whom he is, a squirrel buries nuts for Winter and people, full or miracles. Some, need prayer to maintain a smile. About nature, about wisdom, about why there is darkness that should not be all there is, how to become part of the scene, the one of reasoning about religion and how the pieces of life's puzzle fit, even when they may all not seem to.

Sometimes, we all, clowns or no, need recognize our ways for stuffings life the times that are changing, they become more aware.

CHAPTER TWO

Thoughtfulness in Poems

Love, Patience and Obedience

The gifts of love, patience and obedience are
rewards unto themselves and enough to be sought,
looked forward to and often as can be, they help
everyone fill their needs. And as life gets from
the bottom of the poetic hill to the top, there is.

A knowledge that when these gifts are give, this
is rewards enough. As we turn our clocks to be
awakened to a brand new day, while we learn that
heartache goes away, when times change for the
better is why love, patience and obedience have.

Brought their waters into lakes and geese seem
to be amidst a few swans while children wonder
why they are grown and have children of their
own. I suppose that love, patience and obedience
have been near to be why a scare crow has a hat,
a lion a little roar and

The tin man a can of oil. The lessons we learn
are there for the days of our lives may be a
good planting inside where reality is the soil
that turns dreams into rainbows, the opinions
all become ways to grow and we learn prayer is a
blessing not misunderstood.

Windmills

Doing what should be done, tasks may seem difficult. Count these feats at week's end and remind yourself not to slide nor forget that tomorrow is another day for the proper hour often felt to gather the cotton of the soul and iron mental wrinkles of a prayer for

Peacefulness is a tough lesson to teach when journeys are lost and life seems hurt yet still there is laundry to wash as life seems in need of water and steam and not much of our poetry knows how to be or do everything for our days are there for Jesus to love us also.

So grows a garden of flowering ideas impossible to say much of for how to be is delicate and all asking no questions except being thankful that we have a prayer for our hearts to know where we are acceptable to God as all our being becomes a trust of calmness inside

To help our lives to be acceptable to the windmills nearby and not find anything wrong unless if a hand of a clock falls down and our Humpty Dumpty's could not be put together again and still all and all we learn to be of ending ways then beginning days.

Mind Food

While we love most of life, the professors are many, they are tour guides of the spirit inside, the towers of the mountains where men learn not to climb too high or they'll be dazed and faint when so much is best to imagination instead of taking chances.

Imagine peace everywhere be because one is often alone as time of rest is more with oneself than the day until a nap is there and dreams still with age. Oh, rest continue to be blessings without much to be other than reality, mind food of life, we survive.

One hand holding onto another, a circle is the way we need see ourselves with a blue sky always and cold never too cold to be why the prayers of our hopes and dreams seem more within the mind like a kind of endless circling of days we all live in.

Silence knows it should be of warmth, life has to learn to give, to behold to become an emotion not to be left undone or ashamed for everyday, in everyway, now is found as a place of love for Him. So goes our emotions and so happens our prayers.

Kindly Find Thine Kindle

There is prayer for even I whom whispers turn yells, answers bidding and not a poetic place comes until the minds of men run their inkblots upon lofty skies and whom be one to even wonder why? Why a train is in a

Depot of wonderment, the train of our dreams, hopes and cares as all the guessing of someone might never reach the minding, mending ways until there is more to be than words in books. Oh ye poets: breath and look

Toward the flowers of the fields, yet watch to keep unto the pathway given and let not the perfume be what is not yours to have yet look unto a passing cloud and chase a love until you see life is worthy of thoughtfulness.

Kindly find thine kindle to be and see there is a larger picture than here and now for, we are all kingly when we want to know what shall be, what comes and know nobody really knows. There may seem a sea of knowledge.

In all the mind where fishermen find purpose, reason often a rhyme is caught to be as what is love, a real idea wakening like a waterfall, seemingly seen as branches holding twigs and the sky understands that.

The blueness of the sky truly could understand why a tree is by it's own being a miracle beyond mortal ways and so miraculously nature's manner is sought. The truth is as unexplainable as explained.

Envelope Thinking

Now, on envelope thinking it could be opened for
knowing tomorrow is another day, we all surmise,
try, try and even try all at once to be what is

Whatever. To make a promenade an endeavor of
oneself, loose those emotions that tendency our
manner is what is inside our loves to keep

Out what is abundance with a lot of oneness. So
begins the fortune of peace, honor and finding a
total respect onto the person waiting to be,

The one you see in you, I in I and the hand
holding onto now with a swallowtail in one's
throated song, beak closed and I wonder where

Music comes from. Tomorrow is another day to make
a proper pronoun more, to run around verbs and
to tell why we are all often or

Upset or unhappy by a pout. I shall try to understand
tomorrow what I do not know or understand today
in a kind of way.

Poetry, A Cloud

Not having much of a thought about oneself is to
know why we are all of the same times and to be
with a clock of hours, there must be minutes and
so forth. Often

It's all forgotten where we weary thinkers caring
to explain how much daylight there is, like a
sleeping mind wanting to justify about being
justly fine,

Loose and tight all at once. If I don't feel good
about something, I should move on to something
else and see if that is better to me. What should
matter?

To you is the now while the panic button is always
too far away to use so you improvise and utilize
with a lot of fortitude inside what is to be for

I feel I should invest in more than my emotions
acting up, as it seems every lasting day is still
another to be and poetry is a cloud simple and
kind.

No More Running

And why can't I say of myself I am what I am asking for the moments in my life to rest upon the sunsets I am with liking and loving felt in a kind kiss. The themes may vary, might all go down to the wishing well of our prayers that know how to find all the

Prayers answered. All is fine like when we know a peace is not just inside one lonely man, it is in us all and loneliness can run around no more. Run ahead into the briar patch of love that shows our peace is with the day and night as to find a sunset

And sunrise alone and needing people to be a summary of what is best to be all of ourselves in prayer and silence of letting science know I am what God needs me to be, rich or poor for unto a love, a life one might say we are knowing as freedom to find those hidden

Places in and out and all about not costly for they see us all as what we are and the s unsets will be because of Jesus, because of oneself in Him and He in mankind liking to know living is always a prayer and prayers are in life seeing the morns of running no more.

Feelings

They grow like orchards and groves of apple trees not knowing how for no one knows why an orchard is inside ourselves with each fruit on every tree waiting to be a part of you and I. Looking and being seen from the Skies, people are artists, poets are few and I wonder

What the bottom of a bowl of fruit should be and is as artist's oil meets canvas and words come from deep down on paper or tongue. Yet somewhere they are thought in a waiting kind of way for feelings to be explained. Far into the mind, one sees truth to know how there are

Tides of our lives going out to sea and often return to shore as I wonder, is it our place to only accept waves of feelings or do we think of logic, reasons and purpose of our lives? While innocence never leaves us, when goodness is waiting to be, all may be confusion.

A little proper prayer may need be there to escape the tides and hope for calm where once ways dismay. Let not storms take common sense away and let understanding of our hearts, minds, bodies and souls bring us a real sense of peace even as our mental boat of feelings rocks.

Tee Pee Proud

Indians once, tee pee proud, lives are gone, left in God's wind and rain to make the way clear for what all that was, yet, many a man still lives like the Indian. Hunting for food in the Winter's cold and respectful to the sun and stars of what is best left

Not to be not understood as we look to know and only life's good days can be seen from a love of life and the innermost lights must stay lit so love can be proud also and love of the inner tee pee of memories of thought that sometimes, for many, not seen as all lost.

There are Buffalo herds still and nightingales' songs that give all children hope and respect unto why they need to have a real personality of out-stretched arms knowing of a sea of stars of felt kindness and love still and also in the spirit of tomorrows somehow

There where is today and realities are in a love of prayers for tomorrows asking for the winds of hope to be as proud as the tee pees only everywhere and all was a glimmer of ourselves never to be forgotten like all kinds of songs, chants and dances still felt.

A Sea Song

For there are two sides to every page and a little love, a little jealousy turns people more in love somehow and perhaps a patron of the heart, a beautiful way

To find a new start, a vision of loveliness, a mind full of other thoughts, begun ideas needing a moment to decipher forgiving ideals with special appeals.

Be I a bull thrower holding onto horns, or getting gourd we all can't ever find home. Home is in our hearts, a duty to be everlasting is a

Proper existence and an existence in friendship of goodness as we all find out why there is a boat in a song going out to sea as we listen carefully.

Elephant Hay

Open a door to discussion on the rhetoric value
of window washing versus day dreaming and all we
ever find is we should like, for most moments,
find silence inside.

Even when we meekly talk of the future to be more
of innocence than debate, more of galaxy dreams
than realities open to discussion is a community
chest of our

Own name and purpose for all that give time and
money to reason for liberty to unfurl the option
of what to be, to be what is best like the sword
on a swordfish and

So it would have been so nice if everything were
nice to let the sky be in everyone while a poetic
elephant has his hay and sanity gives way to
happiness now.

Life Matters

When I am hurt, where do I go, what do I do unto the sea of frustration and the despair of years lost in a fury of unexplained hurt with no reply, only deadening silence unto why? Why does living hurt some, why do some seem to be in what is madness, no dream. Not only

Might a body feel pain but a mind may too and life is not always pleasant, as we need not find what to do. Maybe a moment can make life worthwhile, leave a little fresh air in a mental room where stale emotional outlooks were to begin like a spider web of the soul putting up a front

Of not much, there except fear and anxiety now running away because some of us are hurt so I hope this book brings faith where once was despair. Always say a hello to oneself and the only one that knows you is you. A cove inside the mind might be where and how a person

Hides away any peace or hurt or both. We need to get out in the sunshine of our lives and see if physical and mental bruises can heal. If one is hurt, finding a friend may begin to be a new direction of hope and faith. And life can begin to matter if only sometimes.

Oars

Buttered popcorn is no remiss, we all look to make salt for this. We all try to smile when the chips are down and we all seem to know why an apple is no good on a tree.

So, be careful and watch out for snakes. You can make a pie a pie with cinnamon debate about which came first, God or the apes? Why we all make

The price for shoes a purpose of leather, little holes to see through are eyes for feet and every part of me is a sight for your sore eyes. Like a rowboat I am with sanity

Being both oars in the water and a way home just in case I get lost and the watchtower light goes dim. Senses need to be seen so a clarity, a clear day is.

Inspiration

Who is the artist of the soul? Must be the King Jesus or so I'm told.

And who put the clouds above and paints the blue sky? Perhaps

This was God in a quaint way of blessings to be everlasting while the

Opinions of God's place may vary we need to look inside and maybe there is a

Kindness to a special you. We whom collect crosses as well as sea shells

Learn one is more than one seems one be for there is a lantern of light you and I see.

Filling the Heart

Love is too as to swallow an idea and find oneself wondering there is more to life than why it went away while feelings we behold as thoughtful givings.

Reminders of why there is a personable acknowledgment to know what there is to do is to be a loveliness remembering with not only a flower, yet a vase.

Why can't we all put feelings and expressions to the task of filling the heart with joy and let peace be a summary to be lived like a man with a mission to climb

A hill without falling down for with or without growing a little in life's experience and not seeing past now unless you plan out then surmise why a window is open, why a door is closed.

Close

Close, why a floor is beholding to a rug, why a
desk is best to know why a star of the Lord, why
does it shine or does it really

Matter that poetry rhymes, lilies of frog fame
need a name, people look and see themselves, with
every dear moment for Jesus, every envy

Turned loose dreams about waiting for the final
end just like Shakespeare asking what scene is
next until there are no more words to be of

Sorrow for me for I would rather be like windy
ways through the spiritual corners of wanting a
room of rest and peace upon these words I see.

Ugh!

Hurry along, time has her way of ending, but only one song at altitude twelve thousand feet yet we all need our homes, castles are by the oceans front, no place for rest, let's put out the nets, catch those fish, run that

Mile, pull that barge, fill the wagon with sugarcane, now is over, let us all pack for later. Read that jargon the Jehovah's have, may not make sense, neither you nor it. Shell those beans, turn that night into light, look for the planet that is coming

Down, has it been found? Do you speak outer space? Ugh! So do I. What is the sense to all this where people learn and say why the reality of it all is that we all got to get by, find our path, let's be seeing in sleep, see a little of tomorrow's blessings.

Burp

Life need no glory other than living in each day,
no false God nor victory for light is peace, no
duty nor honesty nor decisions when all this has
already gotten it's palace, place, identity and
further past now is where peace is being found.

What might there be when duty has assuredness
with all pens aloud and silent writing need not
begin with weather to step into your own shoes
for words are keenly thought as I let grace be
thine own bread. Forlorned have I been when peace
is not seen, yet

Peers about. Let's not climb poetic trees anymore
for we're all adults. In the anticipation of time,
leave me in rhyme, I give you no riddle except
in wondering why words form thoughts and I do
care to distinguish between mental digestion and
a burp.

Orchestra

A Summer's breeze so cool, almost gone before it's there not unlike years that find they are few left to become a present time. Still lessons of what life is are as endless as they seem only to give way to an orchestra

Made of a few moments supposed to find meaning to people whom have an uncomfortable life and listen to be a part of my time while my senses become full of dreams of what is

Almost all there is but only sometimes for Winter years have often seen snow on my roof. Age puts snow up on my head and I do try to keep up with myself not being greedy or finding that Jesus

Is less than a place that rests, in prayer, in me, for poets be people whom aren't always perfectly seen as their poems for only the room they write in puts a few immortal ideas inside of just what is

Really better read than leaving a person with doubts inside, confused and hurt, I suppose. I share what my feelings say to me in a heartbeat of perhaps, love, Jesus and of both... realities.

Tomorrow

While the days bend into one another tomorrows
might show their slip, seems to be very much the
same like emptying boiling water and finding an
egg. Like darkness seeping in and finding light,
like the

Blues of people having more than they ever knew
they could there is all love for tomorrows heard
today and is a love to be proud of to find hope,
to be a courageous emotional peace as tomorrows

Might look on in the way of a friend needing you.
You never could say of a tomorrow to go away. It's
not even here yet, the vision of a mind needs to
search to find a dream that gives of itself to
be a little

Poetic in a kindness for it doesn't hurt to be
kind, it doesn't have anything yet grace to know
of no disgrace as we are the sum total of our
eternal and entire selves so what becomes of
tomorrow

Is how we make it a day of light today. With
liberty and honor we all need to approach our
dreams and hopes of tomorrow and realizations
will become not the burden of now yet easier soon.

BOB CAREY

Being Thankful

Listen, the windows of the mind are open and there in the distance the doors of the heart are open and both find rest for morning to be. There will always seems not her day to be in sun or rain and making

Sense of feelings so real they just all got to show kindness. To be nice even when you and I say a good-night and windows and doors all but close like reasons being strong to go the prayers we have lived

Not all at once yet a little at a time and being very much thankful. Thankyou Jesus for the part you played in the daylight of our thoughtful thinking, the teaching of how to become one in a new dawn of living for all

Of loving the pathways, God gives us, the honors of mankind bestowed by our peers whom shake our hands in trust of even a better way to help us to know how to understand why the angels of Heaven have our peace

Unto why and what is a wind enough to be cool and calm unto triumphantly turning wrong to right and doing such with all the emotional grace of clouds in the blue skies and knowing inside all is fine, alright.

The Mind's Eye

Somedays I'm going to lose. Seems words don't really matter. I see no way to win when you've already been forgotten, these words that move down a page. Lessons are shades of colors I see, closed be windows, let the

Cold stay away for soulfully we all need invest a few pennies in our poetic piggy banks as the spirit may more for doing this. I may never be away, far from the angel of my soul for in this ancient place I am

And will not laugh nor cry, yet our lullabies will sometimes. For now the river of thoughtfulness is be very wide so I shall know there in the mountains and valleys are promises I can't keep unless the imagination

Finds a place to be why the beginnings are still lit, lit by hopes, prayers and good deeds of mankind's incense of sharing to one another not unlike an emotional child not searching, for love is and the

Solutions may leave, yet in the nightfall of the soul is a songbird outside my window that brings me to see there is goodness near. Winding patterns of the mind's eye might let the hour beseech peace unto what is sincerity always.

A Poet's Window

Be not a decider unto oneself of oneself yet try to be on the straight and narrow, try to look inside before looking for more. Lean unto the lamp post of our being, turn up the stars inside like a peaceful daylight upon the

Wealth of our protected soul and learning the mannerisms of goodness may cause a non-caring tear, yet still a tear that finds there, where the soul is getting tough and we can't find much to be than the freedom that is lost or

Not for life is not best for all. When troubles are gone, the windows are opened for fresh air, the plant is grown out of a dawn that never leaves, yet years do. They leave like a peaceful train loving to be close, waiting to turn

On a path to help us find out why we are. Am I at loss for what to say or a gain in a soulful way? Am I a song unto the sea of words or a wave unto the shore? Perhaps I'll see myself someday leaning on my window's pane.

Reason and Purpose

I keep unto the outlooks of my body, heart and mind knowing somehow the mental roof won't leak; the spirit and soul do stay, not awake nor asleep. We never make much of our lives by just doing what we need to get

By as a nature's way of unexplainable thought seems a prayer is hopeless without Jesus, Jesus needs His people like a song bird his song, a day, a cloud, a night, a moon, a morning, a sun. Awaken to rest ye poems of the

Sea's wave! Bring forth deliberation where might have been an emptiness. Yet give way to a kind and new day free from any storm that might take away logic while giving freedom and refuge to the lonely for He, this He wants.

White laced curtains of the soul, let out the sun, let little light in to still be complete and finding our thinking unto the way we are meant to be, not all the same, yet much of a wind inside our soul sees and seeks

Courage to be with people whom need each other. The complexion of times' windows may change; still there may be a frozen road. All silliness aside, the realms of reason and purpose need a truth, a sense to living.

A Civilized Self

Where be the tear when a plate falls down and breaks for this all may seem sad yet is not much sad for there is glue as I put the pieces of life together by spelling what was and sharing as I need learn how to

Be more reasonable. Lessons of less than plates are finding a rest in an armchair is not exactly all there is. When the light inside one's soul needs to go to expressions touching and finding we all need civilization

So why not start inside with a civilized self. Politeness is searching to see a day to glow in a friend, to seen to be a two-way street of how to begin and never end in a smile that is the most gifted feeling ever seen to be.

We need to get over the bumps in the road and take courage to be a kindly scene as we leave not a trusted truth full of logical ways to be of feelings yet don't let then run away unless it is into the arms of a loved

One's civilized self-becoming more in a complete sphere of respectable, acceptable and trusted love we have and know for a Christian God and a stance for the Jesus Christ that does work in our days and our nights.

Over?

More lessons are in need of positive arms together
with a touching sun and all that may seem to
be completed, done are there when the time is
nearing

And peace is within adding a little wisdom to the
conscious soul always there yet never before seen
until prayer is the door opening. By the path

Wisdom finds love and we all respect one another
until there are few reasons to be more of a
suggestion that can't, for now, begin to be as all

Is seemingly written poetically. Not much is left
except a little kerchief to tenderly find why my
mind wants a book of poems from me. Could this be

For you to read? Do I really have much to behold
more than a fish on a plate and is this a poetic
fish staring back at me? Have I any fish left to
catch?

He Lives In Us

When there seems no place to be, when a soldier felt says a lot for one's head to rest upon asking no more than what is and deep feelings say more than wealth

Could ever be is a church waiting to know inside the lessons of our Jesus. Seems for the receiving and giving is a mention of our thought becoming more one

With the way, God means us to be. As respect to the living and prayers to guide us by the doubts, we have leave. Of our blessings, we thank Him whom lives in us.

The paths of our endeavors leave little doubt, the light within leaves no shadows. Prayers become answered, good will is to be known throughout city and town. Rest seems

To become a place in the soul not troubled yet free to gather itself as a union of spirit and mind letting in love, touching the cloth of the Christ for He is always

There where His love is the forgivnance of prayers as remarkable as the light of day coming again and again. I thank you, my Lord Jesus, for being part of my life.

Speak Softly

Lost are days, gone, yet remembered as love as times can be, all are felt as a smile and all smiles are never forgotten. Somehow, they are like moss on rocky

Beaches often brought home as if to say more of life now because they were and still are even as they rest in the past. While angels with spinning wheels

Go very much quite unnoticed in their giving as I always seem more awakened to find here is someone close to your heart, always and still cares for you.

Loved as for the days I am part of, more often loved and admired, doesn't the spank of life speak softly to us. Softly of special moments, of successful years

And all that is beheld as dear. Of friendships like boats passing one another upon and on the seas of their hearts so trusted, true blue like the sky above with

A sail seen in the wind called soul and the ripples named spirit are guiding us friends to shore as we go to homes of rest and reminding our ways to be

Thankful in a real everlasting lifetime of feelings where time has a place to be asleep in a dream of what is and could be a better place because of Jesus.

Graciousness

Skipper of the heart, guide my pen upon my soul, let me know what should be told, show me a sunset of my bow as I aim for a love not found for there are oceans all around.

Jesus is my live preserver just in case I fall in a sea and needless to say I stay afloat for Him As I ask for a friend to paddle out and pull me to shore, I beg to

Ask for more than being thankful to be found and hope not to be lost again. It is an existence of graciousness I do seek and perhaps I'll pull someone out of the sea.

With courage, aptitude and honor I shall find a duty to grow into a place that I touch truth more for a brother than myself, more for a day than my pages for I am words

On paper and days are the lands of minds thoughtful and real, awakening like a few mountains hiding valleys and ponds with nature turning a page more real than poems

And there is an inward Jesus all about me looking at my soul, knowing I am trying to say more than I k now, more than I see yet with Him all about I try to believe.

Hopes for Tomorrows

Why do we know, my spirit and soul, that there is only one tiller, only one boat. Doubtful as the seas may be, it takes only one voyage upon a page as this to

Light a book, to have patience and let words be meager, not eager, be of bread and butter in the mind not spared nor spoiled and perhaps life will end in one more day

And a good lesson of days is they will not go away. While days have both joy and sorrow, let us find there are hopes for tomorrows. Having a place to know, be

It only a book of poems or a patio to sun oneself. Life is in the finding of oneself unto those hopes for tomorrow that all turns out the way you want them to be,

Sincere, liking of times spent in a depth of original meanings as the realities are enough to know just why we all are learning which way to go. Touching oneself

In a day unspoiled, becoming a giftedness of a trust of a God-like vision is to seek past a manner of what may be seen as a kindness, a glory very reachable.

And Try

Just as there, unto and upon life's tapestry is a
melody unseen yet heard, yet the honor and pride
of one is and tries to sustain hardships life
can hold

As people bail the waters out of their poetic
soulful boats and of course we all learn how
not to cry for with times' eagles flying in the
direction of the

Future we shall learn how freedom beheld by one
and all is a giftedness, a goodness and peace to
be thankful for when changes are sadness's true,
we all need

Those windy days to become calm efforts for
running toward a meaning Jesus has taught of love
with how to know living has a lot. If only our
dreams and prayers

Give forth to become what they are, answers may
be in a love for Jesus while we sing our songs
from our hearts to the realizations that daylight
has much peace and often

There are freedom views of immortality. Giftedness
has become to be why there is love and we all
must t r y to do our best and see past heartache
and unto why love is good.

CHAPTER THREE

Sanity Sings

I like me now. My heart has always guided me. Often I have felt a bruise. Now, I see I am a better man because of the problems I have taken to solve. They have found my heart to pound, my mind explored by honor and love. Honor, the place of inner beliefs never really complete and always taking footsteps to be found. Love, the doors of life wanting to be opened and always waiting to be found.

I don't stop feelings from being heard nor emotions becoming tapered by realities. We never can become less of a lesson than how we really and truly want to be. We need see our lives, to besiege our hearts to seek, see and hope for a little light to help our hearts always be within. Within, where spirituality is a firm ground of mind, heart, feelings and soul all meeting to know how to be to those you love.

All songs will sadly end. Yet, there will always be another of care, truth, love and wisdom. With age, there are patches needed for our mental boats as we all need look for a place to find, a place to rest so our spirituality does not get lost. Words form in the mind and heart making poetic bridges reaching for the spirit that may comply and connect in the soul. Only then, people light up and listen with the might of love and conversations seem more than just saying words. Keep simple words near for they are not high tides that can wash away bridges. They are in corners of the soul wanting to be with the winds at our backs.

Deep down inside the seas of reason lies a bed of pearls where all the fish swim to the sky's sun splashing in and out of their home. Most all of logic need to be made of sense yet felt in a realm of wonderment as if fact was more fiction than anything else. We need to stay in our craft and be sea worthy of storms. Like a few light houses on the coast of a soul, I lend an ear to find out how to be thankful for how I am of my own direction yet placed in a view of others' doings.

Perfect spiritual gains, materials necessities and with a soul that is explaining both lands time to the vast knowledge there where returned kindness seen to open a passage to discover all is the Lords for we are His servants for He is in us. His very miracle may have us believing in Him asking not to be what may not be fair. Yet what is fairness is questionable in a circle of honor, of pride and truth. We are many pearls upon the oceans of thought lent to us for a moment, given to begin to end than a little thoughtful way returns unblemished, a back to the see from they came. So be birth, so be death, to be given, to give.

We look yet do we see what be our responsibility? Innocence has a song in the wind, a praise to know why Jesus is intertwined in thoughtfulness as we listen to the shores' waves of our minds whispering to be why and what is meant to be like a riddle having no words, no answers, just unexplainable as life itself.

The bird on a wire, the raccoon on a porch and I into a page trying to do the best I know. We all show our colors, our tales that may be different. Yet life has a way of catching itself and notice as days turn to sunsets and soon the sun rises. Like a row of corn waiting to be harvested, so is time a clock loosing itself to the farmer. There, where Father Time has peace of mind is how love is inside and all that comes from the meadows of the soul is soon to be a strong meaning. Like peacocks knowing their magnificence somehow is really how we all are sometimes. With a few prayers each day, all I know is to say what I kind of imagine and see a little of as I know goodness is a place wanting to take place. So be the clouds filling the sky, so be the sun casting her light upon all lives.

We all whom we are need one another to gather the day and know there is a wayward wind in our boats' sails there we are waiting to go to the ports of call while our soulful expressions ready themselves to travel unto the pathways and passages of thinking. Reasoning of life may seem song and dance. This be a gift for the giving unlike a poem being shared for Jesus is still alive at least in our hearts. The vast sun of knowledge so written is a more pebble in a pond of awareness just waiting to become endured. The time will come when poets are made and this may behold dreams of wisdom.

Unto the daylight of our hopes for peace is prayer unto the way living is making love and trust all man. We all are many and as much different as the same. Giving a person a chance does good for love of mankind. Now, would be better to appreciate a better day.

Love, the music living give from mountains to seas and all in a real searching way to be why life is a lot at it's best. The inner most secrets give our day's meanings, full of logic showing a truce between what is meant to be and reason to go forth. I may only find a desert to be why poetry is needed as a lizard scampers over this page. There, in an oasis of the heart lands itself to be the loneliest star asking not much, seeing time in a special way, a way to grow with feelings full of peace and all the daylight soon beautiful. Look and seek trust and find another star in the sky, pearls in the see as boats are on course to be why poets live in their poetry.

Sunshine on pages and reasons for rhymes helps people smile and find love inside. The hopes of mankind mended into sweater keeps the winter from being so harsh. While an open heart is where Jesus is, it is with a humble prayer we all need is inside the light life gives. Do what is good for your wordly thoughts to seem like songs and truly life's melodies will gain harmony and there will be peace in the valley of the mind. Please am I to have a mind and let my soul guide me by rivers of life.

I keep my mental bars about me and let the winds blow out my sails with all the inter-reaction of travel from pens to pages trying to be the best they can be without letting go of the tiler that needs me as I need to pray to find helping ways and respecting life more. I plan my days and ways and say prayers that hope will explain life a little better than what was. At least I have tried. As there are elemental changes in us like growing up, there are changes in life reaching in and about to stay on course in an, of course, kindly way.

A page may seem to be very beautiful friend with joy and love pounding prayer within hope and gladness found upon the waves coming to shore once so very far away. Seems life proves miracles really and truly are happening while people pass with smiling faces. Love needs be many ways to grasp a hug helping people when lost find a peaceful shore within, a kindness that is felt within. If people listen to one another, it would be a better world. The stars could shine a lost brighter at night.

Good books are blessings for the soul and put to feelings, here is a prayer. Prayer, like a kite needing more strings in a wind to say what you feel and find more for praying sake to be said. I know blessings shall be found unto the bridges of a logical mind where the eyes of the spirit look all about and around. Pleased to seek a new break of a day so peaceful in so many ways. The fine morning dew is where a thoughtful mind where history awaits a handshake with dreams as lets not to seek more than Jesus may give.

Wonder where the thoughts went, those fleeting moments of time to be very content and recognizing avenues where seas hold a bird by the shoes of our existence, drizzling love all about. Jesus shall soon take center stage to possible reasons where always there like a Mother's smile of opinions leave and love happens. Are not we all people at least the moment we live in, the moments of loving living where reasons to differ and little debates unsolved in the mirrors of our minds?

Perfect may be time and how it reflects us all. Soon, there are mental waves of thought reaching for the very existence of our lives. The light of day is good. One should not be what one is not supposed to be.

There went a cool wind among the forests of the past asking where we are headed. Asking to know if anything is heard like a concert full of nature's oneness in all the truthful beauty of a love for our Lord. Laughter and tears mixed with happiness and sadness leave us to wonder what I am meant to be. Trying to succeed is what I am meant to become, where dreams to see reality protecting my heart and mind from becoming lost or hurt. Safety is a mental island of contentment and happiness may need prayer to see through darkness.

I wonder if a good day has answers and questions kept in us like turning pages of the mind that teach us how to get by? Going to church may hold a clue. Surely, prayer helps too. Be life simpler or complex, be love unto cupped hands, holding water for a friend is a good poetic way of reality, not a stormy place inside.

Calm emotions may give way to a rest, not at all relentless nor distressed is a stepping stone to become of oneness for the days to be. Being thankful for the blessing is a special light of spiritual sky within. I shall grow in an idealistic manner of heart and soul. No matter how many years old one is, there will be a child inside the mind giving youthful where mountains give way to lullabies as Jesus reminds me of me. A day us a lot to have as a special friend is much to find. I call to Jesus, thanking Him whom gave me life. I need an understanding of how to begin to become one person full of feelings in my heart. Here where is peace. A warm feelings worthy of words about how to be where love is dear as kindness should be given and received.

What I question is sanity? Those realms of thought find kindness to be a prayer answered in a moment of peace? We all need prayer of thoughtfulness. Meet peace of mind, find freedom of expression of certainty finding belief in finding Jesus as a major part of nature of our lives. Let's have a humbling hope tomorrows are better because we need each other to help and be helped, to believe in Him.

Let the clouds of the soul cause a cool wind over the lakes of love where contentment is a rippling spirit learning patience and finding goodness. In those days of living not to go away, bless us all and light a candle for a trusting mankind to be to gather wisdom from Jesus.

CHAPTER FOUR

Caring Poetically

Fancy Hats

Innocence of youth, time has a passing ship to get
onto that takes the months to years, that finds
hopes where imagined dreams become more real at

Least in a time where hope is peacefulness and so
we know only dreams might fall but not the spirit
for it is tall as airplanes of the mind not needing

To land for unto and because love shall somehow try
to explain that not everybody is of large pockets or
fan cy hats yet we all must learn to settle for what

We have, to know that we should pray and try to do
better by ourselves if only by making a day of
feelings for others and by being a sacred trusted

Person unto the life one be may be a kind of immortal
kindness of following Jesus and His teachings while
one must believe time does cure all ills.

Dreams to Prayers

While opening up the secret box of the past and
future, both hidden always, I feel glad, I seem
sad, I have no feelings at all for in our depth of

Reason is a little more trusted truth making the
way clear to the unexplainable sky so blue, the
seas so full of life and near us, in our hearts

And minds not unlike a wave coming into sight of
different emotions yet the same tense as a love
for a woman, a love for a song, a love for a

Personal self all day long while we never know
that peace is abound until it leaves us, until
the music stops, the sun goes down yet dreams

Of another day do show the places of living inside
oneself touching the ground and sky and surely it
can be noticed nearby dreams change to prayers.

Black and White

Determination of whom one is, try does all of me
to be right about this, to be soft in my actions,
deeds and thoughts yet firm in what living is all
about. I drink

No wine yet still stumble sometimes for I am
fortunate to have a pen and paper yet realizations,
I think, differ from before that comes when one
is mature and

Knows interpretations find differing places
from one to another and at the end of a page, who
can really say? Not much is absolute and black and
white are usually

Settled for gray as we find that peace is freedom,
most freedoms settle for peace while the day is
soon nearing that a sea will be giving a wave,
tranquil

And calm while the shores of thoughtfulness need
sometimes to be reminded to take their course
in a realistic splendid knowing trusted is what
life is to be.

Because or Why

The truth is a grace, an honorable place to find
there are a lot of our days that give light to
gathering oneself, to know what is right is not
always to try to

To go on even in the darkest nights, even when
hope turns fearly felt and no one can show anyone
how goodness can still be. Because or why the
night is lone, why or

Because the day is hot we all need find out there,
may seem a little joy called sunshine coming
through the window as I catch a few winks only
to find the mystery

Of our hearts is to become here waiting for a
good wayward wind to push us back away from the
rocks near the ocean. Seems all is not l eft in
the rain, seems a lot is near to

A greater self than putting a hat on a cat, than
taking a hat off a cat and wondering if life is
supposed to make sense. Asking of how these words
got lost anyhow, just

Reminding oneself books are basically for shelves
yet what else can there be to help explain the
waves of the sea than travels in the soul of
timeless, meaningful poetry.

A Clear Mind

I do not doubt my goodness nor that I have a clear
mind for I am he whom sees me best, he whom knows
whom knows whom I am. I see my feelings, beliefs

And courage often holding hands with truth enough
to say of more than others can. Confused as even
I can be, I may need a friend to take me upon
the safe shores

Of my soul, a place where I am responsible unto
my comings and goings, unto my days and nights
and hopes are for all of me and you to be alright.
I try to

Seek my mind's manner to be good and I know not
to be influenced by others opinion of me while I
stand on the road of peace still and follow my
will and trusted be

I to whom I am, not left by the shore as a sand
castle waiting for a wave. If that sea's wave does
not come, the castle will remain to be like a
poem filling my

Heart with joy, a prayer to find tomorrow will be
a better day in ever so many ways that depression
is gone and a good outlook finds my daylight to
knowing Jesus.

The Winds

Talk into the winds of the mountains of your soul.
See the trees bend, the grassy hills seem like
seas in a movement of thoughtfulness. Look up and
feel the clouds

As they seem so white and everyday is a miracle
in and about the way life is seemed to be. Circles
seem to be a place in a daylight of our lives
there yet somehow

Unnoticed for we rest in an awakened dream of
knowing where we're going is probably where we'll
be for logic is a circle we know as part of whom
we are. The circle

Of knowing we see Jesus for to guide us, a parade
in a holiday is there to say life is great and a
peace of tranquility giving and receiving of the
bounty nature

Gives to us... here is a little truth in a vast sea
of considerable knowledge. Starfish and jellyfish
all, they are the way they want to be for we are
fascinated

By the sea. Seas often can and really are heard
if you put a sea shell to your ear and I suppose
that there is a lot to know of the winds inside
and about all life is.

An Open Hand and Heart

Renaissance of courage, mind over matter and wisdom is a key that opens the soul, spirit and such truth finds there are paths to the light in oneself to know most

Gifts come from Jesus as He asks little in return. With an open hand and heart, we all are passing one another like ships on a sea waiting for a wave to take us to

Shore. It is with patience, consideration and peace where we need learn of our days, see how they are to be. Becoming more one with ourselves, our ways, often freedom has to be

Seen as we need look into a lot of desires and have some as our dreams. Fields of flowers inside our minds, they are there in case life goes on with unanswered prayers yet

Faith is to be successful and never leaves. Hop scotching from one year to the next may bring a need for new shoes with not much more to be than a peaceful way to be even

As not one prayer is lost. It may be right to hold on tight to one's way setting a course for better days as islands inside the soul even remind us of youthful memories.

Conflict

Thinking I am fine and well, my days are full of goodness inside me as there are few problems I can't handle myself and I seem to function on my own. My feelings say I need

People. There are feelings and reasons to be at patience for the future than to rush or hurry about. While thinking takes second place to feelings, I will remain opinionated

Yet be patient. Trails of living like tears on my cheeks may seem full of love and a lot may seem eternal in thought or true. Yet sorry as a person is, of love and conflicted,

Thinking is too. Confusion of what to say or write at the end of each day may leave a conflict of good and bad needing to be untangled by reasoning to hope for purpose to apply

Yet as many questions answered are more usually to arise. Complexed as a day may seem to be, simple are the prayerful ways of our lives if only in our dreams. We need to find

More than what was past by now, by patiently finding and knowing every bend in the road we are on to someday be a completeness unto our Lord Jesus and part of Him.

The Science of Man

Teach me how to be a man,
show me how to be a child again.
And when I see a large oak tree,
prayer comes to me naturally.
Yet I can only pray inside of me,
for outside of me is more than a large oak tree.
There is God and the Universe and the birds and
bees.

Saying Hello Today

I've lived, I've dreamed, been sickly and confused
so I hold onto faith each and everyday that the
trust of my heart gives me. I find my minds'
seas are

Crowded by poems in and all around and about my
soul while prayers are more there than the food
after for with prayer the fruit of our labor finds
itself to be

Why people know that love is more earned than
grown in God's soil. That prayer is all life may
really be, take praying seriously. Don't be lost
yet find time,

Make time to gather oneself and beliefs for mostly
about the days are to be, the days of newness,
as there goes yesterdays simply and saying hello
today.

A Poet's Pen

Should the day be in me, I in the day or does time give us both our separate ways? While we all seem to grasp onto whom we are, the mind circling the

Soul, touches the waters of the seas and never does forget that an oasis may be many things. The city, the farm, the vallies and forests all add to this

Poet's pen in a view to know God is the master of His Kingdom so let's respect the World we live in. Respect the bird in a nest with each twig found with

Love, so placed. Respect the sky there above us whom gives so much and asks so little. Respect the ground we have to be with plants, vegetables, flowers and

Trees so tall whereas it seems they seem to give so much and ask so little it is the nature of living that brings mankind to believe more in Jesus, the Christ.

Trustingly

A peacefulness of an idea came to me of how to rhyme conversations so interestingly like fruit on trees as neat and clean is a day with rain mysteriously

Making ponds where fish just show up and frogs stay in the sun so much so they may forget how to hop. Must be they're sunburn or maybe got a fly caught in

Their pipes yet all of God's creatures are special and understandance of them is as everyday are many stories unfolding in a clearer picture of ourselves

That can be seen all about the reflection of oneself in clear blue waters as a little stream of thoughtfulness is near reminding me never and a day to grow old.

To Reality Come

Where does my heart begin to be in an infinite
World of poetry? Ask of a little proper polite day
not to change nor go away, to firmly find there
is strength

Inside, to know that all the quotients of being
good and kind might be enough to try to see a
miracle is whom one be. If a door is not there,
one might find

An imagination is a room to enter, a place to
see. To reality come for each one of us is not
the same as everyday has a different pace. Let
God's corn grow

Between your toes, His clouds get in your eyes as
we should never forget that He is love and love
should never be denied. Let peace become a day
of love.

Walls

Self-centered, be the guest of thinking be as I pour my energy into those days waiting and felt somehow now. So I won't leave the way God in me guides me as I meet

My feelings on a common ground where my heart and mind say hello to one another asking the spirit to write a poem. A poet may seem to write way after the poetry is read.

How do I say what needs to be explained? Do we all find life too much and build a wall for our subconscious or simply rest? Walls at first may seem to be a privacy

From what may bother a person and if they are in need of being torn down, perhaps then shall be a cool wind. Walls really need not be for honesty is best a songbird in a

Tree wanting to be heard, not felt alone nor hidden as poems are feelings waiting to break down walls and let one's spirit be about the soul of why we learn from

Our mistakes and we all learn friends we need more than walls that take away a pasture of a wilderness leaving one to wonder what life is meant to be, I think.

Do I Try

Do I try to make sense of words I make or just stand under a waterfall and give description to the feelings of water upon my being? Struggling days may show a little flame of warmth, a calling in need of no more suffering and reminding oneself for how letters form

Ideas and with as much sincerity as a guru inside one's heart we need to hold onto that space God knows where drums go forth and show night's rest as even in an awakenment of day, part of the soul, spirit and mind might or not begin to become a ride in a valley as God

Opens His arms to find we all are partial to loving His son. There are no closed doors nor shut tight windows where wisdom knows no way to be while we all need to find tomorrows better than what was in the little way God meant us to be like an opinion of personal belief not

Really giving way to difference for forces of nature may rain or shine, may seem to return to a logical room of where an apple in a bowl might be left for someone else even if a gift seems lost, should of been years ago, lost in the wind of courageous ways wanting to be again. Best

To be, not to be even lost, while the endless songs and melodies inside bring forth faith and love liking to doves of peace circling the mind and heart, hearing the words of the Bible helping oneself make sense of life and there is prayer where thoughtfulness is always.

God's Dark Soil

I'm so sad, I don't think I can feel even lonely, so hurt in a warrior's society, I don't think I can sleep. The pastures of ideally resting inside truth may always be what one sees in oneself. Tomorrow as belief in

Today is either to have flight or fight where pain is going on and hopes are turned to prayers for all that be because one poet I be might say I believe in decency. There may seem mud between my toes, still I have to clean

My feet and realize there are good days even when living gets too much. While I turn daylight to night with my pen ink, turning pages may grow a tree so proud, defined, wealthy in God's dark soil where love has to

Be noticed, just has to be given a second out of the many miles we travel to find there is a prayer in the way God means a tree to be. Be of branches, shade, nests for bird eggs, a trust liking to see nature asks for sense,

For there seems to be blue skies of peace. Running rivers may see seas near yet what of the trust of a tadpole to wondering be what a frog is? Only a sea knows that reflects as a love enough to give a song, to find there

Is more to nature than can ever be put on paper, ever explained, more that can be is even now. Now a few ideas waiting to take their place inside oneself where schools of knowledge know they are forever changing.

Trust Unseen

Trying to be the best one knows, putting together those puzzles of living and finding people are helping ways to see those gray clouds go away. A person can only take so much grief, so much love lost when it leaves, a poet must

Feel like a tree being chopped away, made into paper and if you see this it may or not seem to be alright, maybe for one moment things can make sense for unto a prayer for a blessing a tree, now lumber can be a house. What can

A house become is a lot yet first comes Jesus and His love. There are many ways to live a life, firstly is trying not to be sad. Pleased to see another day, pleased to be of a kindness even when there is no return, even if the land

Of living has no rain especially when tears dampen my pages. Torn emotions may seem fear yet it takes a prayer to know which way the winds go. The silence of the senses may be yet where is there is trust to be until nature is calm.

Planting Seeds

Why the loveliness of thought may seem good enough at the time there is needed patience and courage to find oneself freer than free, trusted and true as liberty is

Given and one knows one should be thankful. That peace may seem like a stairway going up to the level of completely accepting oneself is enough of a goal. A

Field of accomplishment inside may come from the faith one has inside, the understandance of humility away in the wheat, soon bread on one's table. To be faithful,

To the goodness life is and truly more often an easy lesson is to grasp onto a sober existence is to be sound and fair to oneself and others. Innocence itself may

Seem in need of a lesson. That which is taught is a part of the individual as a gracefulness of how life may seem a dream and become more of a light, a beacon

From a storm. A truth is never completed for there is a God in Heaven. With Jesus in our hearts, most all of a good life can be found as wholesome and kind.

Thought, A Begin of Prayer

Moving violins about silently finding oneself free, noticing not why one is yet for now accepting the light of life like a new day in ever-so-many ways as we look forward to good times like a miner looking for gold and

Beginnings never end. Down, up and all about is Jesus found. A lot may seem a little, a little more than a loft of hay found when a child still beckons the way one is meant to be where a person knows himself, why judgment is

A place in Heaven, why love is a day in the heart no matter how much one seeks the love of Jesus for this is with every heartbeat and knows thought as a begin of prayer. What has to be will be, why the poet sits under a tree, why a song

Bird has all the ideas and it is a feeling there like a sea's wave bringing in the boat and catch while we prepare the fire to fry the fish nearer to the way everyone is, the desire to be full is to receive God's bounty, give thanks

And then perhaps give someone a little joy, peace and place to put his for rest. Seems the seas of living have enough to be for all the kindness not to be overlooked. Even as it may be a great effort to reach out to unseen shores, we try.

Love's Daylight

Opinions have it, most efforts for success in the fields of arts are forgotten or lost in a sea so full of tears I wonder if I need try to say much more. As years pass

And hopelessness is, one as I shall not see much to look forward to. Pens do seem spiritual yet looking glasses go outdated while I do my best to have a responsible way

To say or not to whisper yet listen to the lullaby of the wind as billowed be the pride of going on, forward into love's daylight. Daylight upon a new morn or at least a

Prayer of hope going forth unto a solitude upon a meadow within the hours of life we share with praying ways in so much of a loveliness as to let a rain come and the blues

Leave for my lot is poetry. Love's daylight, talking not of what makes one cry yet opens even a night to light even when candles are what is used to see one's desires

While trusted truths are in a plea to have a fairness of thought given to what is supposed to be life asking no more than why we say often for is not living to be thankful.

Misty Memories

Where memories are like fish jumping toward the
mind's sky where a misty lake fills my eyes and
every year that seems to be doth leave a memory
in poetry like willows on

A mountain tall are now those silent memories
now just thought when the mist is clearing and
memories are there like a smile to oneself, there
are places that are still

And complete as if to say what was is still
meant to be, be like moments of movements of an
innermost medley of why I am, whom I be because
of misty memories. As evening

Lets down her veil with the ease of a ballerina's
dance is a kind feeling taking her place and all
of time is thankful while a cat may awaken one
at the door with a mouse in his

Mouth, quite a doing, as he drops it at my feet
and looks at the refrigerator wanting milk. Then
both of us sleep away the night with separate
dreams of where we've been, where

We'll be like two sailors on a boat of stars that
look down and are pleased soon to become more
misty memories and the dawn is nearing and the
day is soon to be once more.

Proverbial Rose

Struggling wind in mental days finding a rose and seek truth raising winding roads. Life is not a train on circular tracks and words hug to a dug out theme unless they are not meant to be, unless the rain washed out the

Ball game as friends all frown. A sign post and a prayer could lead to love in peace of mind and a jet plane will land. Not on deserted deserts for they are difficult thought like pulling up a proverbial rose has to be a little sacred

And scared when all one be is found in a sea shore of too much to see. See the rose and her thorns are one, alive in the wilderness of their own nature. One need not touch the stem yet clip it or a finger will bleed. The rose if for

Young lovers to take life and their love being careful for dancer's rose may be in the teeth as then it may fall to the floor. Romance may need a rose to give meaning to love and all it beholds. Artists, poets and all might try to say

Of the proverbial rose how beautiful they are in many different ways. A rose may seem to never fade for there in the soul is kindness that was a gift from man to woman to express intentions of continuing thoughtfulness shared.

Where

Where is a word. Where? In the poetry of the mind?
Where is where love be and be where the harps of
angels waiting for souls' fingers to applaud and
become where

The moments are not to be now for where time has
gone is under a blanket of snow waiting for the
sun to show us all where to grow into a meaning
of living where the

Hands of time reach out to see the meaning of
where everyone is a place special to where one
is. Whom does become a daylight inside the hearts
of the mind is he

Whom be holds himself where a song learns to be
more a quest than a question. Where words are
all there are, where truth becomes a prayer unto
faith, we need those

Words to run, to jump about and to settle down and
become a walk upon one's inner soul discovering,
revealing where words were before untold. Where
poems are read, find

Your own poetry where you find you. Be you in a
rose garden counting bumble bees to pass the time
of day or on a aqua blue sea of memories of sea
shells, such is

Where there just is more than enough of
thoughtfulness to make a lifetime remembered by
the sky over those mental seas' waves that just
don't want to go away.

Inside and Out

To think about what is to be, to see unto others
a personality is a discussion of the heart giving
thought to the brain of a monumental momentous
few ideas that

Don't leave until there is a sunset unto the
vallies as well as hills that seem to be of a
kind and gentle likeness so, so great even Jesus
might lose a moment to

Say how life is all about the endlessness of
ourselves in rhymes unexplainable as poetry is
all inside and out. Poetry is in me, about my
breathing, part of my light and

Shadowing words onto this book I think is good yet
know I am better inside and out. These words to
whom it is a concerned whisper briskly becoming
a peaceful place

Unto the lilies of the fields, unto the dried
tears of our cheeks when empty is the pantry of
no more songs are felt by the sun coming in from
the windows of the soul

Is ye blanket so warm inside and out of my being,
here is where poems all finding an end simply put
forth one kindness of a prayer to gather a little
light to go on.

Cross Tears

Free to know love, let thine willow trees have light from the stars, from has to be more a blessing for you whom have kindness inside so cared for by Jesus and,

And feel for the cross can only find reasons to be saved for we all have to live on His land worshiping the way God means us to be, trying to be best to be a reasonable

Explanation of not only good times yet tough times, not only happy times yet sad days. Yet in every tear is a little prayer waiting to be a smile of the inner self

Wanting tomorrows to not come yet take their time in becoming yesterdays. Jesus is our prayer, final, our path full of His love, our opinion not found for it is

A firm ground we walk upon, a clear mind that is full of hearing and vision of the inner soul weather there is sight or listening to the way God means me to be.

Expressions

Further away is the unexplained waiting, searching and looking to find itself and become a poem now scant whisperings of the soul. Because time's hour glass holds

Only sand does not say that is all there be. There are reasons, there are motions life has to know and a beholding emotion to travel over a wordful bridge to seek out the

Right way to be as carefully caring for oneself as artful expressions give way to see the thoughts we all have as days do hold onto our feelings explaining whom we are.

We are unto the sunsets we know, the unconfusing of thoughts of the soul, the dreams turning into realities and everyday reaching out to the next in wonderment. Purposeful be why

We are, those unescapable lights that reasoning shows us all to gather the peaceful ways of honor and respective truth even people acclaim wrong doings and accuse. We whom have

Our feelings unduly hurt need be of a sincerity and proud and trusted if only because one believes in oneself. We need ride the sea's wave to our personal shore of peace.

In light or Darkness

I don't mind being a little lost if someone I care
for finds a note on a music score that helps him
seek the courage to become more of a person to
him and sees there is a thoughtful God for now
is forever, here I am, looking

Out of a window and seeing the past as a concert
of harps in light or darkness for Jesus does
express life well; He is our future explaining
us now. While the pathway seems unfamiliar, when
the daylight seems lost is hope if only a

Knee can be bent for prayer, if only the note one
learns from a music piece brings one closer to
God~ Perhaps some people are impossible yet where
there is life there is hope, where there is faith
in life, living will be for forgivenance.

Umbrella Clouds

Clouds and rain, hand me down my umbrella to be a true keepsake of my heart and mind asking always for another start to gather a few ideas and be headed out to know,

To see why a prayerful existence has shown a way to find why there is rain. Asking ever flower in nature to be of what really matters is a kind smile as I toss away my

Umbrella and grow like a rose that can't find itself until there is shade enough to find peaceful waves instead of too much rain. With effort and struggling, while doing one's

Best, I rope a steer of poetic ways and bring him down. He is a day, he is a night, he is what feelings are when the rains don't go right. We all have to rope our words down,

We all have our peace to whistle a song. Sometimes we smile, often we frown asking what is to seem right or why things go wrong. People may seem judges and judge they may yet

The one is what is meant to be seen in fairness. I rope a steer, not myself, even in the face of others that seem unjust giving out accusations of whom I be.

The Bumble Bee

You can't, in a moment, put your finger on all
the bumble bees of the mind for they are many
hidden down deep inside where warm springs are
waterfalls unto one's soul and with

All the hopes we seem to know, there goes the sky,
a cloud, a spirit passing by. To dream no more,
for a wonderment turns to reality, our faithful
friends, memories, need not

Look to see when there goes a bumble bee. There
is a lot to living, life has many bumble bees and
why here is now, a bumble tells. By bumble bees
that are real and their

Flowers that they have, I can touch that beauty
with a real feeling, with a pen where memories
don't go away quickly yet fly into a private place,
the wonderment only Winter

Knows. Mysteries are many, they are questions no
answers have to be seen. Yet come next Spring the
bumble bee shall make an appearance and dance
about the flowers.

Visual Awareness

Found, the middle eye, the one named the mind
where a leprechaun forgot a pot of gold and all
those dreams and angels have harps to know where
people find a hope and say of life to be this day
where all is even when it is

Waiting for a pathway to take to another prayer
of charmed wealth only prayers can know and give
like a person in a cast of players, no broken
legs, I imagine. The plays on stages are many and
those rhetoric actors are seen to be

The awareness of realities. Times are moving
on and on with an eye on what is and an eye on
what is meant to be. Where poetry is like nature
unspoiled, why poems are singing winds not heard
in a meadow except by nature and her songs sung

Are birds interpreting what is dear and is felt
in a kind of daydream even when seems far away
from oneself, for if you are reading these lines
perhaps you heard a little of nature coming in a
way, good enough for now, til another day.

Ourselves

If God made man, man perfect man,
where would be His sunshine and His tears?
Where would be His lullabies and His tunes
of imperfect time? Where would be His
hearts and His heavens' angels of the skies?
If only because we are of ourselves.

Just Resting After Church

To pretend that love's yesterday is still now, that words in music are really spoken is to say in an explaining way how there, in a heartbeat people see in the dark, people sleep in the sunlight of their soul only to say in ever- so-many ways and days Jesus is love,

The love felt in mankind, the chirp of a bird or just resting after church. To find a place mark, to start again for it is unto this sea's wave logically, building blocks find God's love was always there finding peace is where shores of thought find there, inside a meaningful

Life, to gather truth as sea shells especially when truth needs a friend, even when forgivenance has trust in hopes for tomorrow. While one person paints a picture, be it of pens on paper or oils on canvas, the honor is given out of love and should be, always, done in a respect to knowing

What is best to be done. The mind may seem lost, the soul may seal saddened yet unto the heart, unto the spirit is a step ladder to get down from tears, clear those emotions and see life isn't so sad, f o r Jesus is a prayer unto not only Himself but unto all that come. Come to

Him whom came for our sins to help the night's fear and cold be at least tolerable. So be God's love, so be thought the only way I know to climb up on the step ladder again. Life is not all cherries and flowers so don't expect everything to be great tomorrow.

Over a Bridge

Besides, how am I to be a begin of thought where one dawn of ideas is confusing another where below is a river all flowing like ideas many never-ending as a lake is nearer than one may think and a house is barely peaking in at me with blue shutters answering questions

That have not a quest except to cross and move onward til all the day is felt like blue shutters, like the blue skies that shine upon the lake and warm is a feeling everywhere. Unto the warmth of family felt all the while are more warm feelings seen in an expression of being

Over the bridge always leading to home like a breath of Autumn nearing and goodness is always felt from what is beheld as dearness to love of Jesus as reflections of one's heart is never far away. And over a bridge is still another day whispering inside of how love is.

A Broken Dream

Finding peace, loving life and not a thoughtful
gesture meant is small or contrite yet tomorrow
is a dear prayer to be even when clouds find they
are gray for maybe they must be as rainfall grows
flowers and sunshine also

Is free to be for everyone for the having of a
giftedness that does search to say more and can't
because a broken dream needs glue from Jesus to
wait for more flowers. Flowers in the meadows,
flowers in the fields, flowers on

The window call like all of Christs love that is
everso dear. Yet still Winter breaks the dream
of flowers all the time, for cold is always right
around the bend. Yet broken dreams are mended by
warm Summer also becoming soon

And leaves flowers everywhere with the glory of
Spring. The glory of singing flowers in poetry
and song is when everyone looks to Summer most
of all. The warm emotions that living has, the
church inside sees flowers abound.

The Explaining Spirit

Blessed becomes thine day where age is a place, where timelessness is abound in a song bird of the soul, where the sky is full of white clouds as if to say kindness is as life is unto all that can ever be. Love poems seem to become realities as angels whisperings

Put asleep the night from the day. As I awaken to more, when a calm is to become within my heart, I look for a peaceful energy from God to know a way to greet the way life seems. Seems like music, seems like truthful logic of why peace inside is a goodness for the sea's wave to become a place

To surf until dusk. That the explaining spirit is, that enough is never quite enough, that hope is a spring of dreams often answered is as life still has questions such as who put the fish in the sea and where are there any paths left to take other than following the teachings of

Jesus Christ. Peace, love and charity all find a place for to gather a kindness of giving to one another, to knowing what is a better day. We all need one another to celebrate the good times, to find. there is hope when times are sad.

It may seem not always the best as life's trials and Tribulations can get the best of one and grief will pass but not until peace is made with the God that gave us our ability to reason and to realize He is a God of mercy and kindness is to be even in a sadden need day. We know that our beliefs can become a patch where the soul is torn.

To Keep the Faith

With allness of life itself, with prayers that do come true, it seems there is a God that works in our lives and knows how to put us on the right path when we go astray for He is love everywhere in every flower, in every tree. Because life is blessed, further and onward life is eternal.

Everyone is aboard a boat with Godliness as a paddle and a sea's wave taking us to an island of glory, the glory of Jesus. There is much to do with all of living, with every truth set in a heart of loving He whom finds peace and gives peace freely and gives love He is innocently as prayer can be.

When I have doubts, when I am lost, I find a courageous me to go forth until the light of an inner day comes in my window bring a new trust of myself. Trust, a peacefulness of the skies where all comes to be known as alright. The islands of the mind are freedom, peace, innocence, love,

Giving, kindness and more add unto all this is Jesus guiding the soul and spirit to do what is best and in His righteousness is a day left for prayer, to be at rest and help a friend over a trouble or a doubt by a hug or handshake and rest seems to become like a breeze in a perfect starlit way of

Knowing all is soon fine and alright. As the years pass, we have a hold on being beholding to Jesus and pass a love of faith to a fellowman to carry on, to keep the faith. We all need faith to stay on the poetic boat of courage, prayer and adoration of Jesus, our Lord.

A lot Can Be Learned

While the fabled famous turtle has been in a race with the fast hare, did you know the bet makers had the hare to win so they lost a lot of sleep in the pen.

The poor hare slept and now are empty pockets and a top hat and a cane while he does his song and dance after having a bottle of champagne. He must be sad.

His chance for fame has an ending in a tipsy-topsy way. The lesson here is if you fall asleep in a race you may never get up. The turtle has a lot of pride of pacing

Himself with honor, respectability and trust to himself. Without hesitation, with determination the best of oneself may find a finish line even when lines don't

Seem all they started out to be. Without so much as a song and dance, I must say, a lot can be learned from the story of the tortoise and the hare.

Look Deeper

Doubts, fears and inhibitions many, where did the ghost of thought become, seem lost? How many years do pass until the spirit inside finds eternal rest and do tears stay with the mind I am or find a knife in my stomach so letting my stained greed become forgiven? Forgiven

For turkey, lamb and cod, forgotten all somehow. It may seem life can be all too real, yet unto what is another day, how many hurricanes will come our way? The monsters of the deep may submerge with heads and nostrils snorting flames. The good warrior for peace may have a medal for

Courage when the dragon is beheaded. While love's poetry is the rose, look deeper and there are thorns to behold. Show no pity, run no race for soon life is not a disgrace! We seem that of our duty is begun more' than done, the night will wait for the moon is not full. Where the wolf howls

Now is to her young, where the daylight is found is inside a frown of winds so frigid the rains turn into ice and all the while, poetry is a book on cave now seen yet wondering what cavemen would say of today, of a change, of the glacier that has yet to be only if the sky touches

Earth still. Smoke stacks dot the horizon of the city in fear of more cold in a Winter of snow where mice bites and old mens' pipes seem to be all there is except windows that have snow and so the feeling of living is saddened yet hope still remains like a candle flickering faith.

BOB CAREY

My Heart Is Full

Looking glass, where art thine when all of me
has no rhyme? Sounds of cars, planes and fire
trucks just have me wondering where I am. Shall
my tongue of my mind make me seem too hurt to cry
or make a bad riddle that only says of how many
ways I am a song ended, left in the cold

Of what has opened a can of worms? So I threw
them to the birds. Give me not a word more than
even kindness is a sad word. Give me not a sigh
yet love has only to be one captured moment, one
thoughtful idea, one butterfly. My butterfly net
may be empty yet my heart is full. My suitcase

Of ideas are words there, traveling, like a love
to be freely seen by others like me. I am no
different than an ice cream salesman, a mechanic
or teacher yet where is a pen that knows where to
go is inside oneself, only one knows. Spaces of
time need be in lines as old men and women have

Wrinkles so why should not goodness be inside of
oneself? We forecast not, we learn from each other
why there has only a caring way to find where is
peace of mind. We leave our bodies at road's end
and find and find, with Jesus love has always been
where poets and all try be the best they can.

A Little Light

As is seen, the sea weed of the soul might cause the mind to be in tangled days often leaving one with lack of words, without any truthful ways to even see what is going on, what is wrong. It all may leave scars onto the personality and tears are a luxury that are not found. With any hope

Left in the cold, any song forgotten, it seems all of living is a bottle of wine not worth opening. The prayers of one may seem to make one seem worse for the coaches will pass leaving a splash, the nights will be dark and days will find little light to put in a pocket until an angel traces light

You have for security. Thoughts come and go and how is one to be sure what is best or should become words for the mind is truly a kind of puppet and many are the ways those strings are pulled. Upsetting those hopes, letting ones' ways go unnoticed, sea weed can have a graceful person

Fall and all because the forces of evil might strike a blow. When I die, I don't want anything but my God of Jesus, the son of man to take me to Heaven to have me as I need to make my life a living prayer to be thankful for His many blessings that I have as I believe in our Lord, the Christ.

The Sun of Our Hearts

Surely the morning rain dances upon my window pane and let's all of the sky seem to be alive, like a lovely play's curtain opening in nature's way. There are melodies that behold the windows of the soul. That is where imagined and real flowers grow, frogs in ponds speak on lily pads

While butterflies touch our spiritual skies, all about the mind's eye. Daydreams of better ways to be, hopes of logic to be found can leave a person to smile, not frown, to feel free, to grow, to become someone to himself and find Jesus is within. Softly be our footsteps in the morn of ideas

That let a light from the eternal self-glow unto the soul, help find purpose, reasons and fortitude to grasp unto reality and see past the gray clouds and into the sun of our hearts. The place of rest after a work day is done, the home inside where prayers are without storms is when all

Life makes sense in a greater picture of how we know that God is love and not much more can be told. With all of our peace we learn from Him how there is a pleasant prayer of living life can be, a nicer day inside each and everyday, a better outlook to our hearts for we come to Jesus Christ.

Baton

Due to emotions beyond my control, I jump into my thought hat and seek any corner of an idea I don't know. Roaming in a desert of my soul, finding one oasis being prayer to stop the pain, the heartache, the tears for this desert needs rain for a start. Then let the oasis

Come, the one of security and happiness, the one of love. Bringing a little joyous song inside is letting a peace travel and prayers are answered, freedom is found for God's love is a gift not to be overlooked. As I find my faults need to be changed, my attributes to be clear, I grow with

The way life means me to be. When a peaceful mind is there, where freedom is a heartbeat, until love is meant to a friend, I can only find myself a little lonely yet a friend to my spirit and soul speaking softly of what I now am. People know not why they really are until they are passing

Along their mental baton of personality only to accept someone else's baton and such is age begun, the ways of mortal mankind's learning. If I drop a baton, I must bend over and pick it up, while, I may need to say sorry and start to get back onto life's pathway once again.

More Peaceful

Every corner of my mind's soul, of course, changes and are what I do not know yet needs a little sunlight to explain the pastures of waiting enlightenment. What is truth may seem a bridge over a river and as honesty may not be every footstep this leaves some truth knowing that

It is not so, yet, is the best way to go. To be of many ways, after all, is to be a little beautiful inside the winds of knowledge that were once waiting to be a corner of the find, now passing a baton from what was given back again. Don't forget there, inside the mental outlook, is

A frown looking to smile, a bridge waiting to be crossed over no matter how it seems, even when there seems a worthiness waiting to become an explaining Jesus in my heart. Time has no mercy. It is here, then leaves. I like to find a little prayer to help me to find Jesus near.

I choose no wrong direction yet seek the best way to become even when difficult. Why sometimes the bridges of the spirit may have tears, still the walk over needs be of faithfulness. Then problems that may seem large become little, the days of trouble find answers and one sees himself more peaceful.

Nestled In My Poetry

A song bird by my window, a morning slowly coming,
a reason for rising and a love for liberty felt
always in an awakenment of a dream where a cloud
is felt

In my mind and also is a lofty softness of a
drizzle of what was and will be again in a
carousel of smiling where the heart speaks softly
to the mind and everything

Is fine where I yawn and doze off dreaming of
a day that will show itself outside of me now
nestled in my poetry. With each and every poetic
twig the begin of a chirp is

Felt from afar for the warm sun can only say so
much and parents must do the rest at least until
the young are grown with their own children of
the sunlit ways of

Their poetic homes and all the day needs feelings
not to be completed too much more for like a worm
being pulled from the ground Jesus can explain
the gift of life.

To Rest, To Dream

To be a scholar of knowledge one first needs see oneself. By doing so, an inner sight loves to explain itself, sees cloth and polishes a floor, finds a thought like a key to an inner mental room and enters only to leave. Just do what is best and everything will turn out alright. People

Have their own lives as we all act differently yet still all and all life is forever finding oneself. To help is to be helped, to let the day inside me give way to rest, to dream. Often dreams stay dreams just as a peaceful day is open to discussion of how to avoid the crazy days

That are slept away when so much could of been. Rhetoric songs, all the while, conclude a lot of change as we all need to discover and practice finding the best way to begin a pathway through those? Unlit forests of the soul. They are the unseen wisdom of marching flowers in a way

A place impossible to find nor know until prayers are seen and answered by the daylight of knowing how one whom does divinely struggle to make a home for what is meant to be is kindness inside for what is meant to be. Truly living has a lot to say of whom we all are even when we need pray.

Why Jesus Is Love

With every tear that falls, we look at the middle of life's love where goodness finds itself and asks, does Jesus, to gather good feelings and believe more in them than tears. How many ways are there to interpret life's thoughts? To reach out to a lake of ideas is to be an

Individual, changing sometimes. I see a place in my mind where a mystical mountain goat is climbing where the only top is happiness in a silent love. Books may seem very entangled with truth yet it is how one lives one's life that be why Jesus is love. The love of our days that

Admit to darkness yet light a candle to cast upon our hearts His love. One day by itself may seem very happy or sad. We need put our glasses to our dreams until we find a place where happiness is a sea's wave and all our emotions seem enlightenment engulfing God's love.

Love Is Hidden

Learning of a portrait of oneness of kindly thinking where we all find there is a lot to gain by the oil on a brush of thought with a few feelings put down in why words scramble to be their best as artists share their secrets put down on canvas. Slightly found are smiles

Where the hand searches for a meaning to where a sea's wave touches shore, sun finds land in morn and all of this is reality on a picture often there, no empty felt emotion for love is hidden. Hidden like a cave where treasure is abound and the sea's wave came rushing

In as to say why love is more to be found when one finds an emotion as the shores of thoughtfulness transcribe why we need not worry when love is hidden to be safe for another day as sea gulls fly away and every night has stars giving of a wonderment of why the dreams of wise

Men looking to find peace and love only to realize both are hidden by a seaside of humble beginnings. Artwork of the spiritual mind's sky has few clouds and there are rains that may become storms that leave one as I undone. Yet as peace is found once more, the soul is too.

You May

You may talk wisely in the wind and somebody will always be there.

You may seem to be confused yet unto the wind, the sails will guide, those of the soul.

You may seem out of place until the hand of God teaches a new day.

You may make a prayer seem of a graceful kindness yet it will be of little hope until your heart finds Jesus.

You may talk to yourself yet not hear a word until you find the choir within.

You may search to find an answer and find not until you seek the churches inside.

A New Meadow

Complex intellects, to each person be their own and don't forget to be thankful for love's rosary of

Thought. Scientists are really poets of how they want to be with a formula of how to see a problem and try

To be a how explaining a need. Books might give directions of where to put one's mental hat, how to become aware of

Equations where others have been. Logical bridges need be crossed to seek a new meadow of intelligence often only felt

Yet not completely realized for unto an answer usually is at least a few more questions of searching for solutions.

To Go Forth

Whom be I? A why, a whom or a question scratched in sands asked not to be more than I am? Asking not to have answers, my heart teaches my mind of whom I am, why I have to gather myself for each day and carry

On with a thought of how to be under the sun and among simplicity often, confusion enough to try and hope yet get nowhere than depressed as I take a few deep breaths or find a place alone to go until I collect myself and

Recognize all is better, best to go forth. To go forth following a gracefulness, a kindness and a trust of how life is meant to be, how time is a march of seasons like all the ways of clocks just knowing whom is a dawn is

Soon to be a night and this is to find reasons for why purpose knows how to go forth into times' passing ways and do so with love and grace where only Jesus in us sees a poetic breath of love as we follow Him in undisturbed

Manners for He is the ultimate guide of whom we be while everyone is needed to complete a circle of how to live. Live in the manner we learn to know as loving God and Jesus while it all may take time to learn, to go forth.

Sandy Beaches of the Soul

Contemplate the day by resting in the night. Why this is so is a dream may become real or not. A day might

Be all of a dream, a slice of pie, no mathematics. There is a perfect order to life like galaxies all about.

Slowly comes the inner sea's wave to seem to only sink in sandy beaches of the soul and how this has come to be,

Only Jesus knows. With every question not answered, some bring on more questions of exactly why people dream.

Goodness Oh Goodness

Goodness, oh goodness, play the game fair,
Be in the fair winds of may everywhere.
In every town and every village and in every lake
near a forest.
Let the sunlight in, this life and all aspects may
For goodness you open my heart, take it's toll.
Yet you, oh goodness, cannot leave us.
The times may be waves touching shore,
gone away and left for tomorrow to be a memory.
Everybody says good bye for another day.
Oh, goodness, you just seem to be that way.

Happiness

Happiness is best found when being around people, finding a hobby such as music, walking, reading or television. The best of life is to be open to discussion, to reasoning of self-esteem or religious paths of giving. Take in living with common sense.

Moderation is best, protect yourself from negative people and if you need a vacation find time or learn to smile and be part of the goodness around you in a positive way. Learn to really put yourself in a good circumstance and listen. This is fine, good happiness.

When the warmth of a feeling is there in an inner feeling of goodness is where happiness can be found and we all do need to learn not to frown yet make a joyous pathway to be for an inner breath is where there is a hope, a prayer for happiness. We need share our happiness with

Others as they do with us and in a realm of reason is alot of cloudy days that even when it rains this can not take the goodness of a person's happiness away. Happiness may be having something small as for why, doesn't it seem sometimes everything can go wrong.

Ebb Tides

Ebb tides named the soul are learning how to
become freely found expressions of a heart of
love seen as

A breeze leaving only to be found in an inner
place called logic often there when all seems
lost, hopeless

And confused until one sees a smile and casts it's
glow into a once felt tear soon seen as no remorse

At all, only happiness being seen and left always
to need no more be explained as ebb tides have
washed

All the sorrows of this sinner away and left
one to know much can be explained about oneself
tomorrow.

Every Moment

Left for opinion, where shall this poem go? Will I seem left in a kindly smile or a mess of a way my mind still having dues to give to my heart, my days are emptied and should have love. Time has every moment to go fast

Or slow. In fact, often a butterfly might come by and reminding where the sunset is everything to say, enough to be prouder of now for goodness will leave only to be a begin of somebody else's sea's wave. A wave of a sea,

Be you a memory or a feeling as expressions of know are often of thoughtfulness, I think, are timeless. Weather this poem is right or wrong or found to be in reach of logic, with prayers that influence living, I hopefully

Say I don't want them to go away yet be like a happiness, of determination and find there is hope inside for the lives we be are a *thankyou* to God. Let your body sing in His glory in your coming and going, giving faithfulness

To oneself and so love will be with one's life. Love for knowing what one l earns, for learning of the love of Jesus whom took all He was and cared and a truthfulness of not doubting the love of God in our lives, for it is forever.

A Fan For Summertime

My life is like a book that need not be in print, a beautiful sunset that need not be, a page in a novel read years past yet poetically not forgotten. We are all this and more as we settle for less a pleasure to

Share the days we have for one another by swimming upriver only to be thankful for rest at day's end. While opinion may seem more than it is it usually is not. Not more than a coat keeping one warm or a fan for Summertime.

All the poetry ever to be may not take the place finding more than a canoe slowly finding peace unto a lake where worriment is not about except sunburn. And so be the best of days of rest and logic responding to grace.

The Very Word "Hope"

How do we know, how can we see through an inner tunnel of darkened days, a bedazzlement of hope and a feeling of loss? Standing alone is sad. We need to bring for the light of goodness. The only togetherness there

Can ever be is letting the very word "hope" live in our hearts. Being alone with oneself, is this what reading poems is all about? There are many days in the way life seems that may be lonely and feel at a loss, a

Wondering of what is wrong. People need people. Let people show kindness to those seas' waves so troubles are small and prayers are full of love so everything that was amiss now finds truth is a song not lost,

Yet like a faithfulness found. A poem that not only is like a sunset yet like a sunset found where Jesus is by our side. Seems the fair winds may be better by thanking the Lord so love is the torch eternal even in night.

Sunlit Arrows

All we all of us need be is kindness to one
another. How many places might a rainbow be seen
and how do Gods' arrows fit in a rainbow? The
days seem to have

Sunlit arrows while the night has arrows called
falling stars. With one hand on the arrow and
another on a bow, I suppose care need be taken
to be with God.

Sleep is in the night where angels prepare days
and aren't all people whom love Gods' rainbows
really the same? We all love to be in our hearts,
to know of a

Kinder way be with each passing rainbow, or day!
We all need to express our ways and throw pebbles
in a sea explaining of how nature is all about
our lives.

Mind Lands

Let me say, that in a song, the lyrics often loose. The medley gets lost, the dancing words hold on to

Me as if I were a part of the scene. Due to an idea that died I shall leave this poem to have finality.

Wherever you are, I miss you idea. Life won't be the same. The mind land is at a loss for words to

Say, laughter to hear. Love should be a memory, dear idea, where whom you be leaves one unashamed of

A mind land or a room or a kindness of wiseness of your life, oh idea, what will ever become of poetry?

God Is Near

Having peace is a prayer of love for mind and heart, a daylight coming inside then out and growing in a kind day not forgotten yet let to be why poetry is a firm way of accepting the presents God gives and

Being assured love will survive, love of knowledge, love for life. While there has to be a known pathway, somehow there is light to guide and if the way is worthwhile, when the end of a task is fulfilled, unto

The darkness we leave will be no more there and seem unnoticed, like a night lit with a security so meant in receiving the day soon becomes where worry is no more, left on the run. Then will be peace of a valley where a

Stream divides splendid not unlike the heart must say to the soul: "All is near, all is growth where wisdom is felt from the head to the toes." It may not seem much, to think, but where thinking causes smiles is where love

Rests in the bounty of one's being, in the course of the day, inside the restful night with no more worry, no more fear, no doubt. God is near. Near to the way life is meant to be, love is a songbird in a tree.

Church Bells Ring

In a castle of sand are seas of hands, all the behaviors of children running from Summer to Summer shall have care for even freedom has it's boundary. Were I just of paper turned into words, I'd forget it is inspiration that is

Where kindness has a playground unto a proper way to behold what could become a place to end fear and worry, a grace only the blue sky in eyes so close, church bells ring Jesus is near. Tones, shade, rainbows in rain and

Everywhere is a good feeling that peace is a flag held in one's heart and beheld by the spirit of soulful expressionism of how to be when Chicken Little says the sky is falling and truly it may unless a rabbit gives up a tale even when

He looses at games. Unto this day I give a locket of faith that when a task seems insurmountable, I hold fast to my belief in Jesus and it is with His trust I find courage to go on, to make my life more of an inner hymn of love for Him.

No One Can Explain

Just like peace has all the paths in an idea that time will pass, there are benches along the way to behold our daylight of why there is a lot to be past while it may

Seem most is the future of how we grow, how we know there are so many ways to be. Why not be like one poem to the next and be not forgotten is to receive is to give of how

We learn for life is endlessness in a way of changes in the mind and those stairs will wait to be climbed. We'll never know why nor never know how milk does come from a

Cow. Will we ever know why love is, ever know how pens write poems, airplanes fly and all in a gesture of a much larger picture that no canvas can hold as a picture is a

Few brush strokes, books, a few words yet Mother Nature leaves only questions no one can explain. Explain the sky, how big it is, and the seas and land, how great life be.

Between Ideas

Upon the fall of night, resting peace needs no light. There unto the break of day comes an awareness unto too much to know, let alone say. And what of why the clouds bring shade? Are butterflies seemed part of all is for another day or is there an absolute to take away what

Might of been a feeling of trust in Him? Without a love, a stand on a rock of faith, people would surely not be saved. The climb to Heaven may have bumps in the road yet what if there is emptiness? Would I be loves? Those ideas inside may be somewhere between fantasy and

Fact for where and how and in what way are explanations to be? Poetry may try and some people might see little foolishness where others might sigh unto the wave of a sea seen at dusk. Ask of why, whom can say yet here is to be what was, what is and shall soon become another

Day. Lessons of living are many and history plays upon it's stage while every violin may remind the orchestra to become a love for eternity felt now. Now, where all emotions meet in one's spirit and soul while attention to the loving of Jesus is always a feeling of gratitude.

Each Day

Finding oneself in a pickle, not knowing how it all happened nor where the depth of time has run into no rhymes, only a plain sea of thought not much beholding,

Only those for gotten waves called yesterday that weave in and out of the soul like turtles rushing to sea. Without any of much, less of more, we all go to the final

Sea with maybe those intangibles of love received and given. Enough for Jesus to become even a blessing unto Himself. To grow with one's idea of living may be to

Be like a large oak tree, to have many limbs, many lessons unto the wayward way of finding a little more truth upon the love of praying and being thankful.

Casting Bread

The thoughtfulness of life, what has to be because of this is a lot, now more it seems because Jesus is the thoughtfulness of life. Where love is a child turned

Man, to see himself in his child, to know there is a God whom cares, is a lot of His plans. That every closed mind needs Him to enter and find less confusion

Unto the soul of just what is and is not told for what is best may be seen as breath cast upon the waters of the spirit. Try to see past what is read, be a giant

unto the mind and know down deep the heart to be the guide. Into the sea's wave we have been. Leave a starfish to give back to the greatness of God's melody

For be this now the end of the begin. I pray that there always is another question to every answer found. I hope there are no lost answers yet a lot to think over.

There is Meaning

Blessings to the skies of Christ's way that knows that one as you, as I, need to find purpose, reason to life. The truest gifts may not matter what they be, yet how

We struggle to be free, to gather the meanings that we find and know giving is a song of untold wealth. These words may cup thoughts in one's entire soul, inspire the

Oasis of rest not to be taken for granted, prayers a r e answered when times are sad and do make our Jesus part of our lives. Just as the waves of seas run their way to

Shore, just as there are prayers for peace and love is a kinder time for life as there are friends looking to be in between fence pickets unnoticeable it seems there in

Feelings are the emotional gates always being opening and like Christmas presents under a tree, here seems more is gifts from God, there is a real kindness, a meaning.

Nature's Way

Look for a tree to suddenly say of what is a poetic friend talking as God does in the wind. Without so much as a song is sight where winds bellow sails,

Where the rippled brooks need us to cool our toes, let artists find canvas that needs oils. We never could see why we all need each other until Jesus

Came, until He was a martyr of kindness, until there is a church in the heart for love is meant to be, be there even unto the crosses we bare. With a bath of

Words, with a day unto the year begun I can only imagine how to be when poetry has to be when poetry has no home to be, only brief whispers of life found in a person's

Way of loving God. Love, the endlessness of decades of our emotions hoped to finding peace of mind like a love of a kite in a cloud, a bird in a nest for this

Is how nature is seemingly that way. The way to how one may become proud of living, also accept those responsibilities life has given in a personal way.

A Sailor's Spirit

Grapes of the mind, sweet and undisturbing as a calm wind inside the sunsets of our thoughts, yet to know all thoughts may be best yet some are when someone

Shakes His hand too hard, some cause a sailor's spirit to go off course. Personalities may have personal thoughts. Some are acceptable and stand up tall when

Even if Jesus is the only one that has the ability to help find me in the sadness of spoiled ways and help. When I may grow, discover and find a solution to stay in the

Days of betterment of oneself for often, more often than not we find loneliness even when a friend is near, living may not be dear. One's sail boat might lose the rudder

And be blown to shores of storms inside of a distant land of wondering. We need a solid place within our minds to guide the way, to know which way to be, to go.

Infinite Truth

From the heart of infinite truth to the mind
where wisdom plays her flute is hope for the soul
to get up when there is a fall. Courage may need
a pull or push while honor

May seem many roads and simple might be complexed
felt complexions of wondering how or why that
prayers leave to be actions and deeds. While
opinions are said to,

May often change, the end of a traveler's day may
explain many, what was, heartaches. With all the
views of our oversighted ways, one thing will
remain the same

And let it be rest with Jesus in a moment one
be. Call this moment "eternity". God may be many
things as we humbly give ourselves to see how He
works in our lives.

What Is Best

On top of a mountain, on top of living, see a fish swimming in a river as a little depth of understandance of perception, a lot of truth waiting even when truth

Is on a vacation, a retreat of what is best, a relaxation of principle for ends to meet and a mathematical circle to begin to be complete. Just

Trying to be kind in my wayward winds of actions and deeds, the plans of what to write from one moment to the next and not forgotten is to be what is best.

There has to be a gift of love to grow inside with a trust that the meaning of life shall not, for a moment leave even when hope is behind, lost and seemed gone.

To Find a Way to Be

Since thoughts find love around the bend, memories help to remind us when life was simple and carefree while we lived in fairy tales and let the World go

Round. Without poetic ways to be, we need to find rhymes, certainty and songs enough to know why the angels of the soul are more found with the passing of

Time. Jesus will be in my prayers, finding, showing me where to be. While a lot of truthful days know splendistic are His ways, I like to tide the time I

Have here on Earth and learn to say what is best, learn to know why a dearness of oneself grows there inside the soul while the spirit is in each day slowly found

With daylight everywhere, in mankind and all about. It is by His grace, by His love that times find our peace to always be begun, never-ending in us all.

Lost in Eternity

I find now, unto reasoning, I will not be lost, neither found yet somewhere in the middle of times, some full of goodness other memories lost. I will not cut off my

Nose to spite my face so I need lean over to simply look at the best of times seems they are marshmallows toasted in my mind. They are the crutches of the spirit, the depraved way some of us are, the hopes lost in tear s and with or not nourishment, in a real way, we all feel the same. With one felt emotion at a standstill, another Circles hopelessness, people just might lose their sanity or at least struggle for their identity. Without the blessings life gives, without security or love any sense Life has can be seen like pebbles cast down to the ocean's floor to be lost in eternity. We may all know alot sometimes and forget how to be until we l earn prayers.

A Cloud of Love

Let peace begin with you whom laugh not at anyone
nor calls someone a fool. Finding out, as time
passes, it is not one's face that people look at
yet the hearts

Of the mind, the kindness of the heart and
emotional gratitude expressed in friendships that
do not leave, only grow and reach for a cloud of
love. Sometimes it

May seem somehow the poetic structural movements
of mind and body become very much so in tune with
sight and sound that we all pull one boat ashore
and out of

A sun so hot it must be all for the love of God.
The best of life is found in a spiritual way of
thinking of how we all are brothers, how love is
forever.

Three Jokes by Unknown People

A manager of a restaurant had called it's owner to ask weather or not she should hire a new waitress. "She can speak twelve different languages, which will be good for foreign visitors," said the manager. b "All right, so hire her," the owner replied" "But, sir..." "I knew there would be a but. What's wrong with her?" "Sir, English isn't one of the twelve languages."

Two children are visiting their Grandmother. She says: Go up to your room, but before you go to bed, don't forget to say your prayers. The younger child said real loud, "I want a computer, I want a yoyo and so on. His older brother said to him, "You don't have to yell, God can hear you." "Yes, the young boy said, but Grandmother is hard of hearing.

A ninety-year-old man goes fishing on weekends in a lake behind his house. This particular Sunday he pulls out a frog. The frog said to him: "If you kiss me I will become your princess. The old man places the frog in his pocket. The frog says: "Why didn't you kiss me?" The old man says: "At this age I'm more interested in a talking frog."

The Hopes of My Heart

Without an effort, unto a play, the actors are naked, the day has been lost, forsaken and left in sin. We c limb our own trees, cheerfully, trying not to fall.

It is a loss, to say what is simply seen yet people all are poets of their own desires. Asked whom I be, all I might know, I respectfully submit as much found

As lost. The hopes of my heart aren't an oasis yet endless seas of my retreat to wonderment. Where is my my past? What shall be tomorrow? Need I powder my

Nose or use my will power to make sense of whom I be, to comb my tangled soul out? Perhaps answer s come with prayer and loneliness is a day, one day to be

Over and complete, given to l earn to be thankful to the many blessings for Jesus is the star inside of the soul guiding one along the pathway to understandance.

We All Fall Down

Kindness is the only to be holding hands with serenity. I like peaceful thoughts inside my heart and just know

Truthfulness will survive. The day of judgment will find out where one's peaceful soul has been, where the

Lessons of when it rains with no complaints. Ink on pages, where do I go. Maybe to the logical way of trying,

Doing one's best, being careful. Stay out of sorrow's storm and be happy or we all fall down.

Near and Dear

Pen ink on paper, where will you go for I have just begun to write this poem. The winds seem to whisper

In my ears trying and implying how to behold life as dear. Shall I crawl on all fours or hop on one leg

Or just find never is the r e enough to say. Life has only to rebound a thought, to be in a row of movement

With ones' senses and let them all agree it is where all senses, where religions hold hands and learn from

One another without hurt yet with equal respect and gratitude. As "A Sea's Wave" reaches an ending I think

Of a lot of harmony that has been near and dear to my heart and found in an imagination I had as a child for as

More of reality I've seen as a grown person and everything is better for I care for the days God has given for the

Days God has given to me in a special way. I leave you now with my last poem, "A Prayer" and hope you all well.

A Prayer

The blesses angels of the skies
are here and there and in both thine eyes.

So let thee be pure and let thee be kind
and let thine heart tell thine soul what

Beith behind thine mind.

The End

Nature's Heart

We whom realize our own place is a paradox unto our own being beholds the truth of being by itself and should be enough to me for a decision about my own destiny and where I am, even now

Should or not be where I want my heart to be. Why a flower can be in sunlight, rain and all is poetry away from books. Be I about me silently thinking and wanting to take charge of myself

Still sees my body is a temple so given by my parents and God. There are many lakes near mountains, mountains around valleys and peace about those clouds really not so far away yet how

Does anybody know how or why. Is there a debate that there be no debate? So life is a mystery to me. God must be a kindness of teaching while I stop along the path to rest. Reality, the

Truth of what you believe may always be kept secret. Let the rivers of spirituality f l ow leaving nervousness behind as a fairness of how we all seem to grasp onto oneself leaves our

beliefs proud of the yesterdays of our lives felt in a day. It may not be always that life is peaches and cream, yet the good days make any sorrow, any weight, not seem so unbearable.

A Breath In a Breeze

Now is the page that reruns itself like a breath
in a breeze, like a trapeze in a circus with sewn
nets just incase an inexperience or mistake turns
the artist into flight.

Why take chances, let the clown and his water
flower be the worst that can happen. Let little
flowers be in big hats so minds can say in a
moment how all circus is under tents.

Be I a concealment of logic too sad to say, be I
a belittlement of self, I am going to think about
another day for time may often have very little
to say of itself yet we all have a

Little to do with pride as we see ourselves. Be I
questioning or changing, I am looking inward as
away from myself. To get out and walk not to let
life's cold about is to feel a little

Warmth from living in a candled opera somewhere
giving way to our innocent ways of wondering why
the sky is so blue is to say a lot the Heavens
for truly infinite beliefs of what one

Sees forms our personality as we never learn how
to get up til a fall and need out poetic boats
at sea to be pulled to land, for be I a little
giving and receiving, let me see myself.

The Old Tin Can

Let us sew oats with an eye on the inner self
doing right and letting love cast more light.
There may seem greatness where people look and
don't see and this is not foolish yet

A side of truth not jealousy. Most lines of poems
are all but forgotten as even wisdom may never
be so I take time and effort seriously. Let the
days come and go and let me be

What I do not know yet for open seas and open
skies all show why the boats of our ventures need
to find that island in the mind. A realized star
is where is best to hang our hopes on

As be there religion lastly found, be I in the
bottom of a wishing well waiting for someone to
help me out. There are problems many and answers
few as most of us see in a

Contrite kind of purpose of sense wondering
why the tin can we kicked as a child is still
metaphorically there lying in field like a verb
forgotten and a pronoun wondering what is going
and why we still hold onto the stick we held as
is a,

A quiet, a setting sun or a puzzle with just a
few pieces or a derby hat with a cane or a funny
nose on a face or sand in a pale or a walk along
ocean's tide,

Settling

Somethings have to be checked on as if the race were never over. What be precious are the soulful ways of oneself and kindness of thought. We look to know our way as reality

As breathing in and out of time. I think, I reason, I am and still the days are endless like prayers wanting to be fair. Fair to knowledge and all her endless seas while the

Livelihood of idealistic meanings wanting to become like a folded napkin, a fork in hand. Acceptance of oneself may be a full personality with a lot of spirit for materialism.

The person truly needs little to exist inside, reasons to be. How to settle for a lunch is often to debate to think over what be. Too much happiness or sadness lends a place to

Tears. It is with every innermost candle one lights that we learn to look at the good of our lives. With wisdom and truth answers may be near so let's not give up the ship

Yet settle for looking for peace of mind and don't forget there is Jesus Christ whom answered prayers and knows us even before we arise or rest for we are with Him.

Destiny

We seek courage for the day to be why we are, be it poetry? We learn to find a place to behold our destiny, to have a grasp onto reality and her shores, to gather sands of our existance and giving our prayers to God and Jesus above.

Let some sea shells stay in the beaches of a sober society with our crosses of time seen asking not for what is not to be when every broken dream needs mending by love and love awaits us, at least within, what is to be, destiny.

Be I to desire wealth and fame, be not a tin cup in my hand yet a prayer to give my poems to society for due rewards. Be I to know why there is a road is to find love down inside and count beans for oncely to share, once no more was there.

To make a bed, the night to find a dream for tomorrow and every effort meant in an everlasting way God in us has to give not asking more than the tidings one has to know and giving for someone dear to you with problems also.

Sun Time

Those places we are at, did you see where? Don't move around, the sun will cast a reflection unto our peaceful travels of begin to end of this page if it all really seems to matter as a mouse runs

Down a clock, doesn't he? Well, poetry got the best of me as I milk my harvest of where I've been for seriousness, laughter and patience will be asking not to leave. Yet I must try before my pen falls

Off the page. Those pages, the hours, those words holding on and minutes also leave me to recognize why I am as a vote of confidence to see around corners into those days books, to oneself, know in a sincere

Sort of way as knowing this and the rest of the way as knowing this and the rest of what has been may seem to leave a little emptiness and doubt of the Future for Sun's time may have just a little shade

And a parade of words may seem to take us all into our emotions of love and hate turned into understandance of a better way to be inside these book covers that will soon enough open and close with no regrets.

Trust

Like a see-saw in a dream, tomorrow is after sleep. And when I get on my way, I trust life will bring about a good day. And finding good

And plenty of hope, I see a piano with my ears and hear my mind softly say somewhere, somehow or someday find that ourselves

Here on God's green Earth can reach out to one another in a friendship of the way life has fruit for labor and a quest to be free is life.

Free to smell the morning air, bend down to touch the fragrance of flowers. With all those meanings living beholds I try not to forget to keep a grasp onto

My being, my feet firmly on the ground and earning trust, becoming proud of those tasts that reach out to be seen as a love of doing for not all

One be is easy. Sweeping and mopping then dusting one's room is enough to begin the afternoon as poems seem to relax into a truthfulness of expression.

For Poetry Is

Place a comma where it should be, let a reason rhyme and turn every page in a book only after the meaning has been seen. The night, indeed, needs a place to rest the day's sight into whom we are as if a sparrow were inside me and everything seemed it was just fine.

Ask not for liberty until you have peace within and the political yarn unspoiled yet unrivaled yearns to gather our days to be just a little more trusted and honorable than the youth we all were now simply just left in a plane flying to the most distant idea sooner

Than not nearer to be a begun book like a babbling brook as for even a beautiful sunset gives way to the stars in the night and every poem written expects to be rivaled by the next as 'always' and 'forevers' are tenderly said of why a graceful afternoon may or

Not be a nap all the way into our poetry we have to ourselves... the poetry that is always inside us where no bars can hold us from nature and no fears can keep a dream from being within no matter how lost or found one's mind is for poetry is.

Match Sticks

Bye to the clown suit and hello to a tie as if
there were a dance often dreamed, not yet to be
and heard while raindrops do also dance and so
do the wishing wells of thoughtfulness in a gleam
of musical feelings where a theory knows no shape
or form and

Only a rhyme of how to say is in a way of
manye there could of been more of a peacefulness
instead of fear as every lasting life could cry
as a drunken sailor goes by with a whiskey smell
in his breath and those circles of thought leave
little of the

Days' hours to give up as a poem unto the hovering
night stars and unto a learned behavior or just
love felt like a lot of what lives on and on and on
past the sea's wave and into an answered prayer of
knowing love, kindness and giftedness as a true

Courageousness is a big word when fear needs to be
no more and a lion meows yet there is no more of
laughter until one's pride awakes and the feelings
of liberty match up with simplicity of the heart
unto what should begin and always be a beginning.

Beloved, Respectful and Kind

Escape into a realm of reasoning when perfection needs little forgivenance and the weight of thought has few words and more feelings trying to be brought to light for further down time's road will we be there soon just as once was a poem that made a way to past like a few

Passing ships recognized with billowed sails in the soul. What life's meaning is eludes poetry until a breeze is about and a sea's wave speaks softly of the daylight within for only joyous paths could teach a teacher and so be a school in a classroom or at sea as firstly a

Desk is best and to sit in the mentality of what was, is and could be a kindled flame of winding stairs to be even when they are only in the imagination. We rehearse in a heartbeat of where we are, seek what should be and try to love our society we all are in

And, in some way, a partial place set amidst the sea, clouds and stars. We all know what should be, so let it be so as I think I have an idea of what to do as Jesus's patience is a blessing for the way God made mankind to be beloved, respectful and kind.

Hidden

I think something of myself, and how, as my mind jumps over the moon, while I jump over imaginations and see realities much the same a s respecting the sea that gives bounty and the fishermen have pride to seek all daylight even when darkness seems in their minds. Just a plea,

Not an applaud to find we are all simple to be all we are. Where there is hope, a song of whistling at the sad days until we make sense of our lives and never really know why happens. Why some days are happier than others and as I grow into a past showing the way.

I do not forget to pray as I rest to be more content unto living. Life in a spelling way of itself, mental calm, giving way to trust is finding a lot to be. Trust of oneself to show kindness when all seems hopeless, I pray. Even when all seems lost, without purpose or

Reason is when we all need to get on up and seek a little courage for one more day, always seem, a forever day. People will be people. With all our faults and all our fears, so shall we need one another. With freedom and peace we need to care. Patience shows hidden wisdom.

And There Is Rest

Doing one's best may seem to do well, to remind
there is a thankyou for the talent one has and a
prayer to go on, a peaceful splash of a sea's wave
unto the new morn, unto the days there to be in
a special kindness of why there are few tears in
a reason when one has no

No doubt of how to be, how to act as the curtain
has three acts and the calls leave the actor I am
not an actor yet a person unto all I believe and
think as a poetic string pulls my mind and heart
in a quick solution of how to be for I wonder and
roam little now.

There is no solution that is absolute and there
may seem doubts in all my doings yet I feel deep
down inside I need to go on, to climb a poetic
mountain, to look at the stars and find a love
for every day in a special way. I awaken to greet
the morn and give a hope and prayer

To seek courage to go forth into the inner me
and stay on my knee amidst a windy way of a
kindness, yet a forest, I see as realizations of
the what's and why's to be my guide, to help me
find a daylight of just whom I begin to see as
me, then I leave to see another day.

Now Resting

A slinky, a kite, a yo-yo and skates.. all were a
big game of our past that knew us as we hummed
merrily to the place we are now. We were often
alone, yet content, in rest and learned and were
happy and at peace when simple games we found in
a breath of our love for whom

Is there as a memory of childhood left til now
of a peaceful way not to be real again for there
are skate keys still and ice skates and afternoons
to say so of what will be said of thought inside
where I see memories go forth like sand castles
on beaches and toy jump in

The boxes and presents all where we where we
learned of our ways not to be left out in the
rain. We must of put a few toys at a time away in
a memory for the next time to find soon enough
time teaches a grown- up is near as we see
ourselves with a hat to hang up and a coat

Too and perhaps the presents can be passed to a
friend you see as a son or daughter that is in
many ways like you asking to see a closet full
of games to pass away those days there for the
asking as we grown-ups are now are in way of now
resting of a thankyou, I say.

To Be Free

I am the fortunate day of this page made for
a peaceful reader wanting to find the scholar
he was not anymore found yet forgotten by, of
all things, himself. This is an effort unto the
spiritual sky to unravel what was to help me get
by and complete this poem yet needless to

Say, I am having a little trouble finding a way
to take an idea from the day, give a vision back
to an afternoon and rehearse a tempo of sounds
deep in the soul wanting to get out not unlike a
feeling, a thought frowning, peering and poking
out to be free.

Without much more than a daylight of an idea, the
window of the intellectual self may or not even
begin to be open to say of what is wrong is we
all only pass this way once, that days can be
letters in a poetic sand box weather just a memory
or more an imagination seemed real

For friends whom write for decades of meaning
always meant to be more, always found to be
adorned in a kind and a very special way is like
and of people finding freedom by peacefulness and
beloved memories for so much can be left in an
eternity when coffee and afternoons are shared.

Belief in Jesus

Coming into sight, wondering if the four winds are wrong or right, have to know if there is an answer or if a debate leaves a stalemate. Like a child,

We all kick a poetic tin can down a road inside, deep down inside our soul. While all is calm inside of me now, I seem to be more of a care until I fear

What could be a storm. Storms all tare at my soul, they run in me like a mouse gone mad in a maze, a place to be not part of. I have some feelings I should succeed in

For the four winds have often left me ill. I appreciate my life more, I seem to find the healthy realization that I have survived my difficult days enough to see I am now

Free from the injustice of pain. Perhaps when I remind myself of what was, I will always fear the days that were, those days we find, my Jesus and I, not to think

Of those ill winds yet of tomorrows and the prayers where everything will be fine maybe not understandingly so, yet with a real strong belief in Jesus and all life holds

God is Love

Happiness upon the shores of my heart waiting, looking to become a pathway to Heaven on Earth, a loveliness, a properness and a peace asking the sea to meet the sky,

To seek the courage to continue where we left off... and so happiness comes to be a peace, a freedom for people, a poetic sail full of wind reaching out to know

Why there are tears onto the mind, tears of joy like glasses making everything big. Why a windy day is, why love is alive is the way I want to be. Being

Thankful for the prayers we look to and try to know as times go forth, life should always be a prayer to do what is right, a question always being asked yet

Never found why times seem a little lost, a lot found and here I am unto the morning, unto the dusk of day for here is always a lot to say. Speak of the love of

Jesus, find there are always more together days than mixed up ones is forever reminding yourself God is love, a love so strong one can handle problems of life.

Peace Misplaced

Where are the stars I saw in my youth? Are they gone away? I guess no one can say. What is it we find when years leave us behind our teens and truth

Changes to seem imitation is a something left outside in the rain, left to be a wolf howling at the moon as not much hope is there when we learn only

More rain comes for the days can be seen when hope turns to hopeless unless peace is misplaced with fear leaving and prayer and acceptance of oneself is.

If it is all there is, let the moon be enough to find courage and even drink from a glass, settle for less, accept the gifts life gives and have a fear for the

Unknown yet try to accept not all life is free from thorns, not all times do you go forth for the hours hold minutes, often we hurt as we try to see why.

A Sea Gull

Lacking sense to be of reason and rhyme is to
be like pitching pennies in a wishing well and
becoming lucky inside; truth and peace go hand
and hand. Logic does

Know the way to be on a pathway asking Jesus to
guide when troubled times need a kick in the
rear for then all the days will seem clear. Truly
emotions can seem

to confuse the soul yet the good spirit will pull
one out of a sad place as to learn how to know
contentment again. While doors of happiness, some
sad, open, it

All puts me awake in awe of the inner simple
things as I rest on a poetic bridge of goodness
and cast my line out to find why I am a poet.
Approaching the

Soul inside with a big smile and just maybe life I
be will find trust in a way to lend an ear to the
seas of my explaining my existance of feelings
as a wave is

Gently reaching the spiritual land of reasoning.
Then, back to the sea I go only to be coming in
again while I imagine there high in the sky is a
sea gull flying.

Mind Horses

Looking back, looking up to see the sun yet like my mind, it all seems behind a cloud. The past is over, gone and done so cry me a tear and let's go on and

Onto where the vision of our lives needs logic to behold a single moment that is fine like a path of dirt you and I travel for unto the way of ponds and

Trees are poetic frogs that seem to talk while sparrows make nests in their own way and for me, I don't know what is past for in and about my mind is my soul knowing,

For, personally I care about society more than my thoughts could ever describe. As I struggle to find a prayer to be all mine, I change my mind and give a smile to what

Could never be as giving is not to be asked. Answers, are they not best found inside, hidden on mind horses til the sun goes down, take to heart the best life is.

Our Shores

Survival, let the way be cleared from doubts and let prayers be thusly answered. We, the children of God do grow in His eyes. It must not be said that times

Change mankind for mankind changes times. These necklaces of thought are strong for we need to know how to be good to one another and with our

Prayers. With anything more than poetic ideas, those days we do live in show our shores to help us on our way and hold onto the peace of mind within by giving

And receiving for to care about someone is a two-way street and should not be taken casually. With a shady tree to rest under, a daydream, a lunch and

All the prayers waiting to be and known, the life I am inside of my heart has a thirst for poetic and real adventure in and about the way I am. Should

I not become more one to find a place to gather the fruit of thinking past even time's meaning? While the mind's eye may show us to gather our manners

And restore us to kindness in our eyes to make a place of contently finding a graceful life that is a fully good feeling of calm shores for life is good.

Found and Free

Left alone may seem one's soul, like a reason to
behold yet known are tears of joy to be where is
fear and so a song is freer than we were as my
soul

Runs no more yet reminds me I can't escape my
past so wondering ideas of what to· do are found
and free at last, at least to be. A lot is left
to be free, a lot

Of fear can be in decisions. Dues are here in
what to say, to be and thinking runs by and by
like a mouse in a cage's wheel running around in
my mind. Dreams of

Mice and all the wheel's spin about so this poem
can be written, so the poetry of the soul cannot
be remorseful as we think things over because all
hopes and prayers

Are good to be. Seems a little peace is better
than no peace, a little trust is freedom and so
a gracious day is. A day for men because of a lot
of heart as mice do

Well to be part of thinking in our imagination is
to dream of days hoped to be, be better started
right now and leave those merry-go-rounds of men
and mice is nice.

Better Than Before

There may seem a direct line from our heart to our mind where every impulse catches the soul and shows the spirit to become growing like an oak tree filled

With branches like rivers within asking not to anyone yet accepting the little gifts of life only by giving the bounty nature is as the logic of total awareness

May seem completed only to begin once more as kind rippling ways speak softly. Further into reason, more for purpose than before asks not to persuade the sun

To hide behind the clouds for be understanding of God's Love. How the sandy beaches of day's mind mends our sunburn rests shall our beliefs in life going good,

Good as can be, better than before for with age comes a discipline of oneself, a great day in so many ways to be more of oneness in thinking, more one with Jesus.

While We Love

Persuade me to talk to myself, think of poems,
see liking life as a prayer going on and on with
love as a stairway greatly reaching out. Out of
a star and

Unto the skies of success with wisdom a staff
upon the road of life, a wind in a meadow of the
soul may not begin to be imagination if you don't
think so

While a love for life may be real yet be of care
not to step on wet grass as confusing as it seems
we all learn from our regrets and pass the hour
with a few

Minutes that have much meaning while we love
learning where lessons are taught, where school
goes on even when school is out, even when privacy
has to find

There is courage to being kind, to know tomorrow
may show change, to grow to meet challenges
everyday, to find Jesus is inside of our hearts
and minds always.

Past the Past

There, somewhere well hidden in the eyes of God,
somehow felt in a smile and brought out of the
rain like a lost put is a thoughtfulness no words

Can explain and an effort going on and on to be on
one •s best behavior, to know often time is just
alright yet enough is fine of living so books are

Read to help one by and by with enough respect
and love of Jesus above that to open dues of
knowledge is to seek realities past the past and
into a real

Meditated state of mind where the only bells that
ring are churches and dinner bells for liberty
is silently understood and make no mistake about
whom you be until

Tomorrows are for the change of your outlooks for
as we all learn from living every year we live
we try to visualize that God is a divine teacher
of mankind.

Love Abound

I think I'll write a lovely day and tenderly place it upon these pages like a snow covering a mountain top seen from the windows of the mind, like a nap

on a Summer's day or an afternoon with your thoughts of what, really what is life all about. Why be my minds' sails billowed yet going with the winds of rippled

And sunlit ways set assail in my heart is to reason, to hold and behold my logical place to begin always and once more as endings seem to find they are more if only

Because there is love beneath the stars of our boats that will eventually lead us to the shore to meet Jesus and know all is not lost for people care to find love abound.

CONCLUSION

Of finding a purpose may take forever and a day to explain. Some days you and I may seem a little or a lot lost yet lost to one may be being found to someone else. I will not give up hope. I feel honored to write for the light of day is not only about yet inside oneself, the heart and the mind.

Faith is needed to have and look, here comes respect inside having a normal viewpoint to oneself and others. As peaceful as a light of care, being in a religious way, a hymn of wisdom will always before hidden, becomes real enough to talk about. With no doubt after peace is found. I see life as a gift from Jesus.

Being oneself may never be completely clear. As driftwood comes to the sea shore of hope and faith we need bring to oneself a better day. To better oneself to have a strong love enough to get over sadness so life can find peace and even learn and better oneself. In a prayerful way there are blue skies bringing and showing responsibility of being a little happier, full of joy and peace as the years go by.

Let me say not wrong words yet become good and also profound to see a task and live in God's love. Peace of mind is like soft rains of truth within a precious smile the poetry of nature, the songs in the wind show us hope enough to be thankful for blessings are loved.

Even being thankful for freedom does good to the soul. The nature I see, the birds in the trees, reminds me to think about nature in me. Life may seem sad. When friends are near, where poetry becomes dear, there are good feelings coming. Sadness is no more.

Living on an island is like age and wisdom is. Also to have thought of a spiritual sky is not so far away. The acceptable day gives enough of a soul to have a smile. Nobody can take away my freedom of my love for a personal belief in religion. There is a love in my heart for Jesus. We should have a need for prayer, a basket full of love, a light for our personalities for what is best should be done. Do I move unto the light of believing in myself or hide under the covers to the fear of tomorrow waiting like a snake to interrupt my train of thought? It is by my controversial me to me that I only debate with my knowing ability and feelings never hidden somewhere. There is respect I give to the vision I have is like an eagle in a nest. Let's give nature it's do, then the mind is better also. We always need reinforcement for unto all our days we live in, aren't some as confusing as blessed?

With all our hopes and dreams, there is honor in helping one another get by. As realizations once prayers soon display a oneness of a thoughtful expression of how to be, to find hopes are finding answers and prayers are near. A good blessing is to praise be found as I jump of no worry. Let's give more than prayers, also hopes for tomorrow in a blessing of a song coming or all gone.

Praying on a Sunday morning, noticing you have lived to be in your entering years of age. Knowing why the sun does shine, be why the lakes have lily pads and realize nature is not only about, yet in oneself. The mind may be a forest as we learn of our adventures by being in, about and around society. The awakenment of thoughtfulness should have no end as the reasons.

Sentences are like unfinished prayer. They say what is a need to be showing divine truths, hopes and a lot of daylight. To make sense of life is to everything and ideas to need to be is to live within a realm of goodness not to forget one is loved. Faithfulness always and forever has not an ending. With a zest for life and feelings inside, fears leave and forgivenance becomes strong. Let a trust be inward and a mirror not caring an imagination too far because being alone is not all the time to be. Let's be communicating not with oneself but with others. To become at rest, keeping problems small and keeping alert is best and answers are along the ways ideas of living.

The peacefulness of a cloudy day may come from the prayer of a friend. If all those ideas of the way life seems were given to you, what would you do? If everyday had a little truth for you, what would times be if say hello to your heart and look for courage to on when your mind just can't make sense of life's meaning? There may be a lot to do, say, think, write, acclaim. Without love, it may go away. When one attains peace of mind, contentment has to it a courageousness to be where feelings soon words of finding meaning to life that gives shade to the soul. The soul, like walking in a park looking to find oneself. These blessings are finding how to give and receive a moment of reflection of good memories, and having some with prayers that free the soul and confusement will not come. Take time and mistakes are small.

To start again, to find a certainty to one's life of being close to God and to dream is what we all have. Peace, freedom and fairness to others is what I look to know. "While kindness to oneself is often we live to be in a understandance place to see a giving of patience and carefully love others. Look at people for the good in them not a flaw in character like inhibitions are. We all start out perfect and it is a shame some are unfair. No one has the right to jump to conclusions. An empty person full of grief, may need a smile. Put a safe idea away deep inside oneself and see it through like a song, waiting to be for the singer within become feeling.

Let me put my head up high and know there are clouds inside life's meaning ways. There is a silver lining in life where prayers come through by peaceful effort. If seems the love of Jesus in our hearts where He gives us prayer through difficult times. Let's leave our feelings of guilt, anxiety and frustration be put to rest and not be lost for tomorrow might find answers to our prayers. Understanding oneself is more than words yet feelings deep down inside and not taking for granted blessings we know that guide us along our pathways of our lives. Our silence often speaks louder than words. Give a *thankyou* for the love your family gives.

We all have dues to pay. God knows there are many undercurrents that rip at our soul, that teach us to gather the memories that are good and find freedom of expression enough to begin to heal any mental wounds leaving upsettings behind. It is only be the confessions of sadness to that relieves heartache and pain. Life when hurt should think needs be made sense of. By gathering oneself to be free, to know there is a silver linin to every cloud, to see the entire picture is to forget sadness and be thankful for the good moments and see how liberty knows there is an answer. Prayer from the heart is a way not to be lost.

All anyone can do is try to understand, make sense of oneself as we replace those troubled ways and think of a very overlooked word. That word I "love". The land of the mind is to keep sacred. The end result may be why some upsetting ways are. I remember true friends matter more than emotions. A brick wall I am not. The enemy one has is fear troubled times can go unresolved. Bewilderment takes a dedication to the spiritual side of life. Nerves of life can break. Any beliefs of decency to others is to pray for their resurrection and togetherness of body and mind.

Let innocence by the mirror s of the spirit and soul with love of Jesus pointing the best way to become. When people care for an ailing person more than oneself truly both shed a tear and that God's love will hear where salvation is near. A pathway out of troubles is to look at days past finding the blessings of gifts oneself and other is a prayerful way to find oneself. Goodness is a trait often difficult to find like a challenge to bring down the moon and stars finding life gets better as time goes on.

Printed in the United States
by Baker & Taylor Publisher Services